MW00442966

Building Wealth
Buying
Foreclosures

JOHN W. SCHAUB

JOHN ANDREWS

New York   Chicago San Francisco Lisbon London
Madrid Mexico City Milan New Delhi San Juan
Seoul Singapore Sydney Toronto

ISBN: 978-0-07-159210-9
MHID: 0-07-159210-5

This publication is designed to provide accurate and authoritative information in regard to the
subject matter covered. It is sold with the understanding that neither the author nor the publisher
is engaged in rendering legal, accounting, or other professional service. If legal advice or other
expert assistance is required, the services of a competent professional person should be sought.

*—From a Declaration of Principles jointly adopted by a Committee
of the American Bar Association and a Committee of Publishers*

McGraw-Hill books are available at special quantity discounts to use as premiums and sales
promotions, or for use in corporate training programs. To contact a representative please visit the
Contact Us pages at www.mhprofessional.com.

This book is printed on acid-free paper.

To Valerie, my partner, copilot, and best friend.
You have brought balance and joy to my life.

Contents

Contents

INTRODUCTION

Many real estate investors will take 10 years or more to achieve their financial goals because they pay close to retail prices when they buy and they pay retail interest rates when they borrow.

Buying foreclosures gives you an opportunity to supercharge your investment plan by buying well below the market and financing at better-than-market interest rates. You literally can cut in half the time that it will take you to meet your goals if you improve your negotiating and borrowing skills.

When lenders have many loans in default, they will make deals with new buyers that they would never offer to the original borrowers. These great deals include lower interest rates and payment schedules. This provides an opportunity for a new investor to buy at both bargain prices and on great terms. These great terms allow you to buy with a nominal down payment and have cash flow on your investment from the first day.

Buying a foreclosure has a stigma: that you are taking advantage of another. The truth is that anyone in foreclosure has a problem that he or she doesn't know how to solve. If you can solve it for that person and buy his or her house at a price that allows you to make a profit, you will both be happy with the result.

Any lender who is foreclosing on a loan or has a borrower who cannot repay a loan also has a problem. It may not be as personal a difficulty,

Introduction

but the lender too is motivated to solve the problem, and, when approached in the right way, it will help you make a good deal.

I have been in business of buying property in the same relatively small town for more than 30 years. During that time, I have bought dozens of houses in various stages of foreclosure. The sellers have all been relieved to be rid of the obligation to pay a loan. If they could have sold their house to another buyer for more money, they would have. They sold to me because I was the only buyer willing to buy and solve their immediate problem.

Many of these sellers were days or hours from losing their house in foreclosure. Although they had months of notice that they were in jeopardy of losing their homes, they waited until the last minute to take action.

Some of these houses were in the nicest neighborhoods in town. Houses in foreclosure range from the least expensive house in your town to the most expensive. High-income people, who often buy the most expensive house they can afford, get in trouble, and in bigger trouble, than those with less income. Often the best opportunities for making significant profits are in the better neighborhoods in your town.

When a higher-income person is in foreclosure, it is generally not a tragedy. It is a setback. That person is often well educated and able to rebound quickly and rent or buy another house, if he or she can just get rid of this one.

When a lower-income family loses a house, it is a more serious problem, as they may not have the resources to buy or rent another house. They are at risk of becoming homeless. The good news is that a buyer may be able to help them avoid a foreclosure and give them enough money to rent or even buy another house.

The neighbors will benefit from you buying a house that often will need some attention. If the house is empty and no one is taking care of it, it becomes a neighborhood nuisance. When you take possession and begin making improvements, it improves the neighborhood.

Introduction

Foreclosure scams become common when the real estate market takes a nosedive. Many foreclosure services will appear. Some agencies may be trying to help homeowners in distress, by counseling them about their finances and helping them to negotiate a workout agreement with lenders. Others are simply trying to make a quick profit.

Unfortunately, desperate homeowners often are open to desperate ideas. Some have written large checks to a "foreclosure specialist" who simply kept the money and never did anything to help the homeowners get relief.

This book on foreclosures is unique because it shows you many ways to solve a foreclosure problem other than by just writing a check.

Many homeowners have existing home loans with low interest rates. In addition, they may have a significant profit because prices have increased since they had originally bought the house. These houses can be purchased without paying off the loan. Many lenders will be happy for a stronger buyer to take over a loan when the market is soft. This gives you an opportunity not only to buy at a great price but also to take advantage of the existing low-interest-rate financing without paying the costs associated with a new loan.

Building wealth is about more than just making money. Building wealth is building your reputation, experience, connections, information, knowledge, and credit. Even if you lose money, if you have this other wealth, you can regain the money in short order.

1

Getting Started Buying Foreclosures

Probably you have never purchased a house in foreclosure. Most likely, you have been bombarded with reports of thousands of foreclosures and heard about the great bargains available. You may think that getting involved with an owner in distress will be messy or that the effort necessary to negotiate and close is not worth your time.

In my 35 years of investing in real estate, most of the houses that I bought were in some stage of foreclosure. Certainly, my best deals were. In addition to buying bargain properties for our account, I have been able to help many homeowners save some of their equity, find another place to live, and avoid a foreclosure on their credit report. Some sellers were just one month behind, and others had not made a payment for a year or more. Some houses were bought directly from a homeowner and others from a lender.

Building Wealth Buying Foreclosures

Just as every property is unique, every lender has its own policies and personalities. A lender eager to get rid of a property will sell to you at a discount and even finance for you. However, you won't know that a bank is ready to sell at a major discount unless you make it an offer.

In this book, you will learn how to buy from both owners and lenders. An owner may live in the house or have had purchased it for an investment. Lenders don't buy real estate for investment, but they may own property on which they have foreclosed or may still have a loan that they don't want to foreclose. Knowing whom to talk to, when to make an offer, and how to negotiate is worth thousands to you on every deal.

There are many different ways to buy a foreclosure; some require a lot of cash and some require none at all. I have actually been paid by sellers to buy their house. The amount they paid me was not a commission. The sellers actually wrote me a check to take their title to the property and to take over their loan. That's better than a nothing-down deal.

This book is not for everyone, but it will be a great help to you if you want to learn how to buy one or more properties at bargain prices. If you are new to real estate investing, read my first two books, *Building Wealth One House at a Time* and *Building Real Estate Wealth in a Changing Market,* for an understanding of how to make money buying real estate. The chapter that follows will cover what you need to know before you start the process of buying a foreclosure.

2

Foreclosure Facts

The following are some facts you need to keep in mind before you invest in a foreclosure. Ultimately, they will save you time, money, and perhaps keep anything unfortunate from happening.

1. *Not every foreclosure is an opportunity for you!* In fact, most are not opportunities that you want to pursue. It's a mistake to look at every property that is foreclosed in your town.

   Any time that you are presented with a foreclosure opportunity, stop and ask: Do I know enough about this property to make money on it? Do I know how to rent it or sell it? If you answer yes to the first question, ask whether you like it enough to own it for five years.

Your plan may be to sell the property within a five-year period, but sometimes buyers don't appear when you want them to and you have to wait longer than you planned to get your money back. You want to sell your property when the market is hot, so that you can get a high price in a short time. Getting a good price when you sell is as important as getting a good price when you buy. Many buyers negotiate great prices when they buy, but then because they have a big profit, they sell for a bargain price to the next buyer. I've done it and have watched many others do it. When you have a large profit in a property, you are more likely to sell it for a lower price than you could otherwise get for it.

2. *Foreclosures are everywhere; you only want to buy good properties near where you live or work*. Identify one or more neighborhoods where you want to buy. Make that decision based both on the history of appreciation in a neighborhood and the potential for future appreciation and its attractiveness to live in, either for yourself or for a tenant. Learn values in the areas that you have identified by looking at property that has sold and is for sale. My two previous books, *Building Wealth One House at a Time* and *Building Real Estate Wealth in a Changing Market*, cover in detail how to select the right neighborhood.

Try to buy in neighborhoods where there are few rentals. Good tenants want good neighbors. Buy a good house (well built, well designed, and well maintained) between two good neighbors (people who take pride in their home and neighborhood) and you will be able to attract a great tenant. Before you ever consider buying a foreclosure, you should think about what type of property that you want to buy, what price range, and what you will do with the property after you buy it. Answer the questions: Why are you buying? Do you hope to resell for a quick profit? Do you plan on living in the house? Do you plan on renting it and holding it as an investment?

Foreclosure Facts

3. *Gas is expensive, and your time is precious; research before you get in your car to look at a property.*

4. *There is a lot of information available on the Internet.* Get on the property appraiser Web site (search for the name of your town, the state, and the property appraiser) and here's what you can learn:

   a. What the owner paid for the property and when

   b. What their neighbors paid and when

   c. What the properties are assessed for

   d. The ratio between land and improvements

   You may be able to read the actual instruments that are recorded, like the deed and mortgage or deed of trust. If you see a sales price that seems way out of line, it could be a transfer to a family member (the sales price may be too low) or it could include owner financing (the sales price may be inflated).

   Also, look for a Web site hosted by a local Realtor or your Board of Realtors who will show properties currently for sale. Search for "the name of your town" MLS. Because the owner has not sold, you can assume that most of these prices are at least a little above the market. You may also be able to find sales statistics on your market, which often show the average and median prices of houses sold and sales broken down by size and price. Also, there may be information on the average time on the market and the percentage of the sales price at which listings sold.

5. *Be careful not to confuse making a bad business deal with char-ity.* You will meet sellers with serious problems. One seller in foreclosure I met had recently lost her husband, and then her child became seriously ill. Anyone would feel very sorry for this woman and want to help her. Unfortunately, her house was not one I would want to own.

When faced with a situation when you feel sorry for the owner and you are at risk of paying too much for a property that you do not want to buy, stop and rethink the situation. If you buy her house for too much money, then although you have helped her, you have hurt yourself. You may lose thousands of dollars on a house you should not buy. When you find a seller who needs charity, take out your checkbook and write a check as a gift. It is far wiser to make a gift to a person in need than to buy a house you don't want or to pay too much money because you become emotionally involved with the seller.

6. *Buy only properties that you know how to manage and want to manage.* It's very expensive to learn to manage after you buy a property. The mistakes you can make, like renting to the wrong tenant, can cost you several months' rent. I recommend that you read Leigh Robinson's book *Landlording* for a good basic understanding of tenant management. For a more advanced course, see my Web site www.johnschaub.com for my full-day course "Positive Landlording." Learn to manage first, then if you have the time you can practice and earn some money by managing someone else's property (work as a manager), then if you like it, buy your own building.

7. *Management of an apartment building or commercial building can be like running a dairy farm.* It's a 24/7 job you cannot walk away from, and it's nearly impossible to hire good management for a fee that will allow you to make a profit. A building with several demanding tenants can be a full-time job. If you already have a full-time job, beware of buying a property that will consume a lot of your life.

8. *If you plan on buying and selling for a short-term profit, know the market for selling before you buy.* Houses of a certain size

in certain price ranges are selling far more quickly than your average house. Know which sizes and price ranges of houses in your town sell fastest, then go one step farther and learn which neighborhoods have the best track records for fast sales. If you can buy a house in the right price range in the right neighborhood, your chances of selling quickly are greatly improved.

9. *Only buy properties that you actually want to own for a long time.* Don't even take a bad property if someone tries to give it to you, and some people will. Some properties cost money to own even if they have no debt.

10. *Anyone losing his or her home to a lender is unlikely to paint and clean on the way out.* If you have ever looked at a foreclosed home after the owners were forced out, you have noticed that most of these properties need a lot of cleanup. Owners may do irrational things on their way out. A good inspection should reveal the items that need attention.

11. *There are different times in the foreclosure process when you can buy.* Some take more money than others. In Chapter 5, you will learn the best time for you to buy, given what you want to accomplish.

12. *When it's easy to buy, it's often hard to sell.* In a seller's market, sellers will make it easy for you to buy—too easy, sometimes. You must know your market if you plan to sell or rent—before you make your offer to purchase.

13. *Bankers become more conservative as more loans go into foreclosure.* They will instruct appraisers to be conservative with their evaluations. They will reduce the amount they will loan and require better credit from their borrowers. A bank will base the amount of its loan on the value or what you are paying for the property, whichever is less. It often takes about a month to close

a new bank loan. If you are buying the house of someone who needs to close right away (like: this week) or lose the house, you need to find an alternative to getting a new loan from a bank. Several alternatives are available.

14. *Fixers-uppers typically cost more to fix up than you think, and it always takes longer to fix them up than you planned.*

15. *Not all houses are worth what it cost to build them.* Some are over-improved. Many people spend too much fixing up or building a house. Be careful not to base your offer on what the owners have invested in the property.

16. *A foreclosure may not wipe out all liens.* A foreclosure or trustee's sale only extinguishes the claims of those properly notified of the sale. If you are a lien holder and not properly notified, then your claim is still valid and secured by the property.

17. *The Internal Revenue Service (IRS), even with good notice, may have a right of redemption.* Although that right is rarely exercised, any money that you spend on the property during the initial 120 days is at risk if the IRS has a lien.

18. *Some states use a judicial foreclosure process and other states use a nonjudicial, trust deed sale; some use both.* Both can yield the same results. A judicial foreclosure requires court approval, and the process can take from a few weeks to well over a year. A nonjudicial trustee sale often takes a month or less, depending on the state and the system in which it takes place. If your state gives lenders a choice, they will choose the nonjudicial foreclosure because they can foreclose much faster.

19. *Bankruptcy can drag the process out even longer.*

20. *You can help the seller by buying his or her house.* That person will still have a credit problem, but not the foreclosure, and you may be able to pay enough for him or her to move into another house.

Foreclosure Facts

If you take the responsibility for making the payments on the loan and begin paying it on time, that person's credit will improve.

21. *When the market is soft, it is a far safer strategy to buy and rent than to buy and sell.* Often, the rental market will improve during periods of high foreclosures. People who lose their houses need a place to live, and after the foreclosure they are a better credit risk.

22. *Buy within 20 minutes of where you live or work.* Closer is better.

23. *Making a good deal on foreclosures takes knowledge and a little patience.* Buying any property takes time, but as foreclosure owners are in crisis, it takes a calm buyer who knows how to make an offer that the seller will accept to put these deals together.

3

What You Should Know Before You Buy Your First Foreclosure

Why Buy a Foreclosure?

Your first question may be: Why buy a foreclosure? There are a couple of reasons for doing so. The first is obvious, you should be able to get a bigger discount when you purchase from a seller or a lender who is anxious to sell something. The second reason may be less obvious. A lender who has a loan and is not receiving payments is open to offers that reinstate the loan or, in some cases, renegotiate the terms of the loan. In other words when you buy a foreclosure, you can take advantage of the existing financing, and you do not have to get a new loan.

A real estate investor wants to be in a position to buy quickly whenever she finds a great deal and then to hold and sell only when the market is strong. Although, there are many more foreclosures in a buyer's market, when property is hard to sell, than in a seller's market, there are always foreclosures. Good deals are made in every market. Great deals are made when the market is soft and someone has to sell in a hurry.

In a hot market, sellers get many offers and lenders have more business than they can handle, so neither are likely to make many concessions. In a soft market, the sellers will often give large discounts off the price and lenders will cooperate, as they do not want to own any more property.

When you are able to buy at a discount and get the lender to cooperate, you can buy a lot of property without much money. If your goal is to own 10 free-and-clear houses as soon as you can, then being able to buy houses at discounts ranging from 20 to 50 percent and with existing financing will knock years off the amount of time it will take you to achieve your goal.

Should a Beginner Look for a Foreclosure?

Although a foreclosure can be your first property purchase, some experience negotiating with lenders and sellers will give you a big advantage. If you have purchased another property, you have had some experience. Any negotiation is by nature adversarial, with everyone looking out for his or her own best interest.

Before you begin investing you should be on solid financial ground yourself. Do you spend less than you make now? An investor sets aside part of what he earns every month for his future. An investment is an asset that will grow and pay you in the future. An investment goal to accumulate assets that will produce more income than you need to live on is a goal of financial independence. Owning a group of houses in your town that will appreciate over time and produce income while they grow, can make you financially independent in only a few years.

A Substitute for Money and Credit

You don't need a lot of money or perfect credit to buy property. That is why more people have made their first million in real estate than in the stock market. You can buy a house worth hundreds of thousands of dollars with nothing down and rent it for enough to pay for itself. To do this, you have to buy it at a discount and borrow the money on good terms and be a good manager. These skills can be learned.

Although stock investing can be profitable, it takes more money to buy $200,000 worth of stock than it does a $200,000 house. Time, effort, creativity, and courage have always been a substitute for money and credit. You can buy a house with nothing down by taking over an existing loan. But you need the courage to take the risk that you will be able to find a tenant who will pay enough rent to make your payments, or a buyer who will pay you more than you paid for the property. You can find someone who will sell you a house with nothing down by knocking on enough doors or sending out enough letters. You can talk a lender into letting you take over a loan if you find the right lender on the right day.

Having said that, a little money in the bank will give you a cushion for any errors you might make when buying a house. If it takes longer to sell or rent than you planned, or if you find something that needs repair, then a little cash can come in handy.

How Much Cash Should You Have on Hand Before You Buy?

How much cash you need on hand will depend on both your comfort with risk and your plans for the property. You, as the buyer, determine how much cash you will initially invest in the purchase. Your offer will state how much cash you will put down and the terms of any financing.

If you have little cash to work with, then you need to make offers that require you to put only a little down.

In addition to the down payment, you will need enough cash on hand to make the payments on any loans requiring them for at least six months. If the market is exceptionally slow in your town, plan on making payments for a year. If you get lucky and find a buyer or renter in a month or two, nothing is lost. If, on the other hand, it takes many months to find a renter or buyer, you want the cash on hand to make the payments so that you are not under a lot of pressure to take the first offer that comes along.

Finding the Right Foreclosure to Buy

There are many causes of foreclosure. Simply borrowing on terms that one cannot afford to repay; having a job loss, illness, or marital or family problems; or experiencing many other situations can trigger a financial disaster that leads to a foreclosure. Sometimes a change in the financial markets will cause distress. When prices fall, or interest rates rise, some homeowners will stop making their payments. The press may report a great increase in the number of foreclosures. Recognize that when property values are climbing, there are often only a couple of foreclosures a year in some towns, so any increase will be a large percentage increase. Often most of the foreclosures are concentrated in certain areas of a community.

A Street Called Financial Disaster

An example of concentration of foreclosures occurred in my town. One builder built and sold 18 houses on one street, all to first-time homeowners.

Most of these buyers were able to qualify for a 100 percent loan, so they had nothing invested in the house. In the first couple of years, more than half of the homeowners stopped making their payments. These homeowners who had nothing invested thought more like tenants than owners. The results were predictable.

Unfortunately for the neighborhood, most of the foreclosures were then purchased by investors who rented them to tenants. The price that the investors paid was far less than the original sales price. This depressed prices on the street and depressed the neighbors as their property values dropped. It was the beginning of a downward cycle as values and the appearance of the properties declined.

Although it would be easy to buy a house on this street, I would advise against doing so. The houses on this street will attract bad tenants, and property values will continue to decline, for years. Although values may eventually rebound, you will probably give up before you make a profit on this street.

There are foreclosures scattered throughout your town. It is far better to buy an isolated foreclosure on a street where most houses are owner occupied, not on a street plagued by foreclosures. The owner-occupied houses are more likely to be sold to users who will maintain them better than a landlord would, and property values will have a much better chance of increasing.

New Houses Often Have the Financing Costs Built In

Many of the subprime loans that default are secured by new homes. When a builder sells a new home and helps arrange the financing, the sales price will typically include the financing costs. The resulting high price is more than the market value of the property.

Included in the loan are things that wear our fast like fancy appliances, floor coverings, paint, and landscaping. Two years later these items have little cash value. When a builder sells a new house requiring nothing down, buyers don't tend to haggle over the price, so they end up paying more than the house is really worth.

When the market slows down or prices drop, some of these buyers will simply walk away from the house and loan and move into a cheaper rental. They are more interested in this month's payment than the long-term potential for appreciation and debt reduction. Look in an area of new homes that were sold at high prices with nothing-down terms and you will find a lot of foreclosures.

Be careful buying in these areas. Prices will typically decline until the marginal buyer loses his or her house in foreclosure. They will not begin to appreciate again until owner-occupants displace the investors who buy the foreclosures. As long as there are a lot of rentals, property values will not increase.

Understanding Values

Knowing what a property is worth is an important first step in making an offer that will produce a good deal for you. When markets are in flux and prices are increasing or dropping rapidly, it is a challenge to know what a property is worth. Protect yourself by buying only one property at a time. This is called "cost averaging."

At the top of the recent market, I bought a house for what I thought was a bargain price. It seemed like the market stopped the next day, and even though I thought I had bought a bargain, in fact, I had paid too much. Fortunately, it was just one house and not a dozen. Unless you have years of experience and a healthy bank balance, let "one house at a time" be your mantra.

When a market is at its top, many people pay too much and many builders build too fancy and too big of a house for the market. Just because someone spent $400,000 building a house does not mean the house is worth $400,000.

Case Study

A seller once approached me with a file full of receipts. He had documented every dime he had spent building his new house, which was located in a nice part of town. Unfortunately, he had overbuilt the house. That is, he had built too much house for the lot. His house was bigger and fancier than every other house on the street. Although he spent nearly $400,000 building the house of his dreams, the market value was only a fraction of what he had invested. We eventually bought the house at a large discount, but even then we had trouble marketing it. Overbuilding is a waste of money. Be careful not to buy an overbuilt a house or overimprove one yourself.

When evaluating a property, you can't just look at the square footage and calculate a value. You have to look at the rest of the houses in the neighborhood, and make sure that the house you are evaluating is not out of line with those houses. When I build houses to hold for investment, I purposely build a little smaller, less fancy house than all the other houses on the street. Now my house will get a little value boost as the other, more expensive ones will pull my square footage value up a little.

Cycles in House Prices

House prices follow somewhat predictable cycles. The cycle is influenced by both inflation and the amount of money most people borrow against their homes.

We all know that a dollar today is worth far less than the same dollar 30 years ago. As the government has not adjusted the currency for inflation, today it takes about $10 to buy what $1 could 30 years ago. A movie ticket you could buy for $1 in the 1970s costs $10 today. A gallon of gas that cost $0.30 then, costs $3 thirty years later. A good car that cost about $3,000 in the 1970s costs $30,000 today. None of these things are worth more. The dollar is simply worth less.

Houses are priced accordingly. A $30,000 house in the 1970s will cost about $300,000 today. It may be the same exact house, but the dollar has dropped in value.

A chart showing house prices through the years would look like this:

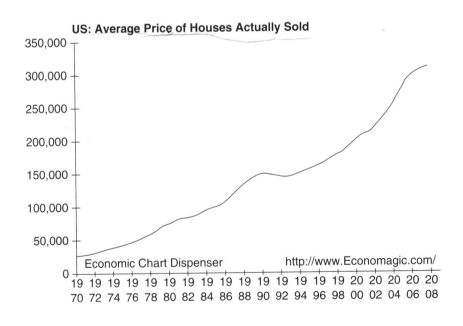

US: Average Price of Houses Actually Sold

Economic Chart Dispenser   http://www.Economagic.com/

What You Should Know Before You Buy

The rising part of the chart is caused by a combination of inflation and increased demand. The flat part of the chart occurs when demand slacks and the market adjusts. Houses that hit the peak on the chart may fall in price, but they will be supported by the previous plateau.

4

Making the Most by Buying Property That You Understand

Unless you buy the right property, you won't make much money buying foreclosures. You can buy a property for half of what it is really
worth and still lose money. I once bought a parcel of land from a bank for
less than half of what the previous owner had paid and half of what the bank
had loaned on the property. It seemed like a terrific bargain at the time.

After more than a decade of trying to sell the property, I finally gave
it away (literally) to a local nonprofit organization. It was a mistake that
not only cost me a lot of money but took a lot of my time. The lesson I
learned was not to buy a property about which I knew little, even though
it was cheap. Some property is just hard to sell at any price, because
there are few buyers. Buy a property that buyers and/or renters will want
today at some price.

Here are reasons why some property is hard to sell or rent, which are
easy to identify.

Avoiding the Big Three Losers: Bad Location, Bad Design, and Bad Construction

Bad Location

In the residential business, a bad location means an unsafe or noisy or a high-traffic street. Most people just don't want to live there. A couple of times I have bought a house on a busy street thinking that perhaps it would become desirable for a commercial use and become more valuable. Those houses are still houses 20 years later, and someone has had to put up with a high-traffic, noisy location for those 20 years. Good tenants and most buyers have choices of which house to buy or rent, and so the houses in bad locations will often go to the ones with no other choices. Don't buy houses on busy streets; they are too much trouble to rent and sell.

Declining Neighborhood

Neighborhoods are constantly changing. Brand-new houses in brand-new neighborhoods often start a slow decline from the day they are new for several decades. Older neighborhoods may become more attractive because of their location, the size of the lots, or just the price. When neighborhoods begin to run down, often many investors buy properties and renters begin to outnumber owners. At some point, the properties will begin to be bargains and users will buy them and fix them up. If you can find a neighborhood that is in this part of the cycle, with owner-occupants replacing renters, it is a good time to buy. These cycles often take many years, and some neighborhoods never seem to change composition. Study several neighborhoods in your town to see if you can spot a change in a neighborhood. If it's changing for the better, look for an opportunity to buy.

Making the Most by Buying Property That You Understand

Bad Lot

Early in my career, I sold lots for a residential developer. Some sold right away and others were harder to sell. Eventually every lot sold and had a house on it, but there was a difference in their desirability. The difference becomes less obvious once you build a house on the lot. But, some lots are still better than others. Because it is the lot that appreciates (not the house which is wearing out every day), you want to buy the best lot available. Look at the lot closely. Is it a normal shape? Does it drain well? Is it in a quiet area? Corner lots often require the house to be built a minimum distance away from both streets. This often results in a very small backyard. Walk around the house and make sure that the yard is adequately sized. Always look over the fence to see what the neighbor's house and yard (and dog) look like.

Bad Neighbors

This may be the hardest problem to fix, so it is always a reason to pass on a house. Neighbors who will not maintain their property or who create disturbances in the neighborhood will depress property values and scare off good tenants. Unless you can buy their house too, look for a better location.

Bad Design

Most houses are built by professional builders who are smart enough to use well-tested house designs. Some homes are built by nonprofessionals who have done the design and building themselves. If you notice a custom design, it may be functional and attractive, but be on the lookout for things you find unusual. Strange rooflines may require extraordinary maintenance. Large expanses of glass or a poorly designed second story may make it costly to heat and cool. An inspector may say the house is in good shape, but use your common sense and ask the question, "Would

I live here?" I would be willing to move into any house I own. That tells you that both the house and the neighborhood are "normal."

Bad Construction

Unless you really know construction, hire an inspector or have a friend who is a residential contractor inspect the house for you. Some houses have chronic problems like a settling foundation or design problems that are too expensive to justify fixing. You might argue that if you can buy it cheap enough, it's worth fixing, but remember that you will then have to invest your time and money to fix it. You will make more money buying a house that is already in good shape at a bargain price.

Management Disasters to Avoid

Some properties require a lot more of your time to manage than others. Managing a motel or rooming house is a full-time job. Managing a commercial property, apartment, or duplex is a part-time job. Houses rented to long-term tenants require the least amount of time.

If you already have many demands on your daily schedule, it is a mistake to buy a property that will require a large investment of your time. The end result is often a sale of the property at a reduced price because you are tired of management.

An old joke is that most apartments and commercial buildings are sold because of illness: the owners are sick of managing them. To the uninformed, it might make sense to have all of your tenants in one building. I managed all of these types of buildings and one thing is certain: The closer your tenants are to one another, the more time you will spend trying to solve their problems.

Making the Most by Buying Property That You Understand

Owning houses on different streets not only separates your tenants, it diversifies your investments and gives you safety. More than one commercial property owner has lost money because a long-term road construction project limited customer access to his or her property or a competitor had built a better building next door or across the street. Houses are a totally different type of investment.

Unless you are an experienced real estate investor, you need to learn more about all these topics. I suggest you read my first two books: *Building Wealth One House at a Time* and *Building Real Estate Wealth in a Changing Market.*

5

Buying at the Time When You Have the Greatest Advantage

Market Timing: Recognizing Cycles and Buying Smart

Although it is impossible to predict what is going to happen tomorrow, current events identify the part of the real estate cycle that you are in now. Identification is fairly easy to do if the market is moving steadily up or down, or if it is flat. Tops and bottoms of a market are harder to pick.

When the market is going up and prices are rising, competition increases and buyers move fast, sometimes creating a buying frenzy. This is a great time to sell, but if you buy, you are likely to pay a retail price. If the market goes up after you buy, you look smart. If you buy at the top of the market, you may pay more than a house is really worth.

When the market is going down, it is hard to pick the bottom, but doing so is not so important. In a declining market, few people are buying, so you have little or no competition. This allows you to take your time and make offers at a price and on terms that virtually guarantee you a profit.

Tracking Bank Foreclosures

The press and some Web sites report the number of bank foreclosures, so you can track the trend. When the numbers are increasing, more properties will come on the market at lower and lower prices. The number of foreclosures, even in a soft market, rarely exceeds 2 percent of the number of houses in an area. Often the majority of these houses are clustered in certain neighborhoods where marginal buyers are concentrated.

When the number of foreclosures bottoms out, it will take a while before prices begin to increase. Builders are not creating new inventory when there are a lot of foreclosures. When the inventory of houses decreases, prices will begin rising and buyers will outnumber sellers again.

Tracking What Buyers Are Bidding at the Sales

Just as important as the number of sales at foreclosure auctions is the amount at which houses sell for in relation to their loan amount and real value. In a hot market, properties often sell for more than the loan amount and sometimes more than the real value. Although there are fewer foreclosures in hot markets, there are always foreclosures.

Suppose a property is worth $200,000 and the loan amount is $180,000. At a foreclosure sale, the high bid is more than $180,000. The lenders will know that they can force a foreclosure sale and recover their investment.

A year later a similar property with a similar mortgage balance brings only a high bid of $150,000. If the lender accepts this bid, it will lose $30,000. If the lender doesn't accept the bid, it will get the property.

Knowing whether lenders are recovering all of their money at foreclosure sales is important. When they are, negotiations with them are more difficult. When they do not receive their full amount at a sale, they will be easier to negotiate with before the sale, as well as after.

The key to making big profits when buying foreclosures is knowing when the lenders are ripe for low offers and renegotiations of their existing loans. Lenders differ in their willingness to negotiate. Some lenders have many high-risk loans in default and are very willing to discount or renegotiate those loans. Others may have few and be less willing to discount or negotiate. Even a lender with only a few bad loans may be willing to make a great deal on a property that it does not want to own. The only way you will really know the willingness of a lender to accept an offer today is to make an offer.

Timing with Lenders: Getting Information about Lenders

Lenders are rated by the government and private rating systems. Using the Internet, you can check on the financial condition of a bank. If it is in poor financial condition, it will be more likely to make you a great deal.

Testing Lenders with Offers

The only way to know if a lender is willing to accept a low offer is to make one. Decide what is most important to you, the price or the terms, and then make an offer asking for the price and/or terms that you need to buy the property.

If it is public knowledge that a lender is in financial trouble, then when you find a property that is owned by a lender in trouble, make an offer even lower than what you could possibly expect the lender to accept.

My rule for making offers to lenders is to write down the offer that works for me, and then make a first offer to the lender 20 percent lower than that amount. More often than not, we buy at a price within that 20 percent range.

Timing on Particular Streets

After you identify a neighborhood where you want to buy, begin walking the streets in that area and look for opportunities. Talk to the neighbors and ask them if they know of anyone who wants to sell. Look for properties that are abandoned or untended. Both of these are signs of financial distress and could identify a foreclosure.

Sometimes a bank or other lender will have a for-sale sign on a property. Some brokers specialize in selling bank foreclosures. Learn who they are, and look for their signs.

If there happens to be several foreclosures in the neighborhood that you are working, keep track of the addresses, notice how long it takes for them to sell, and do research to learn the prices at which they sold.

Buying at the Time When You Have the Greatest Advantage

The best time to buy is when the number of foreclosed properties begins shrinking and the prices begin to increase. You don't have to hit the bottom to make a great deal. In fact, the house that you buy is more important than getting the very best price. Identify the one that you want to buy and then be ready to make your offer when the street begins to show these signs of recovery.

Timing with Homeowners

Making an offer that a homeowner will accept has a lot to do with when you make the offer. Many homeowners go into denial when they can't make their payments: They assume something good will happen and that they will not have to move.

As the sale date approaches, some homeowners realize that if they don't sell before the sale date, they will have to move and they will have no money with which to move.

Although your chances of having your offer accepted increase as you approach the sale date, it is best to meet the sellers and look at their house as far in advance as possible. Then you can do your research on the house and get your financing lined up so you can make an offer and close on it quickly.

It is likely that the homeowners will be approached by several buyers and have received mail from many others before the sale date. If you have met them and talked to them about how you might be able to help, you will have an advantage over the others.

About 10 days before the sale, you will want to go see them again and make an offer. It will take a few days to either renegotiate a deal with the homeowners' lender or to close with other financing. You have already done your research and have your financial arrangements made, so you are ready to move quickly.

Your Personal Timing and the Finances You Need

To buy a foreclosure, you need to have the time to research and negotiate the deal, and have your finances in order so you can actually close the deal. Often investors bring me good deals that they have negotiated but cannot close because they don't have the money or borrowing power in place.

As the market softens, it becomes harder for investors to borrow money. If you know that you are going to need to borrow money to close a deal, you should have your source lined up before you make an offer. Often you will have just a few days to close, so you won't have the time to identify and close on a loan in that short time.

There are several possible outcomes when you look at buying a likely foreclosure.

1. *You may be able to simply take over an existing loan and begin making the payments on it*. That will probably require you to have enough cash on hand to meet these obligations on an empty house for several months, plus whatever amounts you may need to clean the house and make needed repairs. If you rent this house, you may still need to add some cash each month until the rent increases to a level where the house can repay the debt on its own.

2. *You may be able to renegotiate the existing debt*. That may require you to make up the back payments and pay some costs. Or a lender may ask you to pay down a part of the balance on the loan. This could take a cash down payment of 10 to 20 percent of the loan balance.

3. *You may be able to negotiate a new loan with the existing lender*. If your credit is good and you are able to make a down payment, the lender may agree to make you a new loan with the proceeds paying off the old loan.

4. *The lender may just want out of the deal altogether and give you a large discount if you just pay off the loan.* That will require you to have enough cash to pay an amount equal to between 60 and 70 percent of the loan balance, but it must be all cash.

5. *If the property goes to foreclosure sale and you want to buy it at the auction, you will need an amount equal to your bid, which may be 50 to 70 percent of the value of the house.* You cannot make your bid and then go get a loan; you must have the loan first, which is one reason these properties sell at such a discount.

6

Preforeclosure: The Way You Can Buy with the Least Amount of Cash

What Is Preforeclosure?

Before a lender files a required notice publicizing a foreclosure sale, there is a period of time when the homeowners are falling behind on their payments, but only the homeowners and the lender know about it. I consider this the preforeclosure period, and it runs from the first day the homeowners discover they are in trouble until the day of the sale.

At some point, the lender will advertise the sale. After it is advertised, the foreclosure services will make a list of the homeowners' names and sell that list to hundreds of subscribers all over the country. When that happens, the homeowners will begin receiving letters and postcards.

You have an advantage before the lender advertises the sale and the sellers' names become public notice.

Finding Sellers Who Need You

Homeowners who cannot make this month's payment, or who just missed last month's payment, will not even consider themselves to be sellers. They hope to find a way to keep their home, and some will. Your job is to find the homeowners who need to sell because they have no other way to save their equity and their credit.

When you are able to find homeowners who are only a month or two behind, you are in a position to both help them recover some of their equity (if they have any) and protect their credit. If they go through the entire foreclosure process, they are unlikely to get any money from a sale, and their credit will be damaged. The result of damaged credit is not that they won't be able to borrow. It is that they will have to pay high interest rates when they borrow. With a foreclosure on their record, all their credit charges will be higher, and they will be stuck paying much higher payments for everything that they finance.

Talking with the Lender

When buying a preforeclosure, a major advantage is that you do not have to acquire a new loan. Rather than paying off the existing loan or getting a new loan, you can negotiate with the existing lender to assume the existing loan on terms that work for you. If you can't negotiate terms that you like, look for another property with a more flexible lender.

If a lender has few foreclosures or if foreclosure auctions are bringing high prices, then it may not want to renegotiate the loan. However, if the lender does not want to foreclose on this property, it will welcome an offer from a buyer with better credit than the current borrower and with the ability to make the payments.

The lender's decision will depend both on the real estate market and the lender's financial condition. Some banks or other lenders will have few foreclosures while others will be swamped with foreclosures. Your ability to recognize which lenders are willing to make good deals is important if you want to buy preforeclosures.

If you are not sure about the lender's willingness to make a deal, simply make an offer. If you can start a conversation with the lender before the file is turned over to the attorneys to file the foreclosure suit, it may be easier to get to a decision maker.

When a bank or any lender forecloses, it is required to start writing checks first for the attorney's or trustee's fees, then for insurance, taxes, and maintenance. Multiply the effect of not receiving payments on a loan with the requirement to start paying expenses and you can see that a lender's cash flow has taken a dramatic reversal.

Case Study: Cash Flow Swing with a Foreclosure

I am a lender, and during down markets I will occasionally have to foreclose on a property. I would much rather renegotiate with the current borrower, or make a deal with another buyer who wants to buy the house and will take over the loan, than foreclose.

The numbers tell why:

Original loan balance	$225,000
Monthly payments	$1,800
Taxes and insurance	Paid by borrower

When the payments stop, instead of receiving $1,800 a month, I now have the following expenses:

Monthly payments	–0–
Taxes and insurance	$3,000
Attorney's fees & costs	$2,000
Mowing, repairs, etc.	$1,000–$10,000+
Advertising	$1,000–$3,000+

In the next six months, rather than collecting $10,800 I have to write checks for at least $7,000. That's a minimum difference of $17,800 from the anticipated cash flow.

A private lender may not have the reserves to survive if she or he has several bad loans. A bank may have a hundred bad loans. A hundred bad loans of this size would have a $1,780,000 impact on the bank's cash flow. Look for a lender with multiple foreclosures that are not being purchased at the foreclosure sale and you will find a lender who will negotiate.

Before You Begin to Negotiate with a Lender

It is important that you have a signed contract before you begin negotiating with the lender. Because it is not your loan or your property, the lender has no reason to talk with you. Talking with you about the status of someone else's loan would be a violation of the original borrower's rights. However, if you have a contract signed by the sellers to buy a property that gives you permission to contact the bank, try to negotiate a payment plan that you like. Now the bankers will talk with you.

I find it helpful to have the sellers in the room with me when I make the first call. If you are routed through a phone answering system, the system will typically ask for the loan number, the last four digits of the Social Security numbers of the borrowers, and sometimes the date the last payment was made. If the borrowers are there, they can furnish you with any information that you need.

Often lenders will make a deal with a new buyer that they will not make with the existing owners. This may not seem fair, but it is reality. If you make a good deal with the lender, that same good deal may not be available to the current owners.

The first step in this process is to get the sellers to show you their entire file on the house, including the correspondence with the lenders. This correspondence will often give you a contact person at the bank and a telephone number. Use the toll-free number if they give you one, because you are likely to be on the phone for a while.

Getting the Information That You Need

There are two reasons to ask the sellers questions. One is to get information. Don't take their answers as the truth: Check their statements. For example, if they say that the house next door just sold for $300,000 but that their house is newer and larger, it is easy to check that statement for truth.

Even if the neighbors sold for more money, you might want to inquire about the terms. If they sold for cash, then the price reflects the market value. If they sold on terms, they might have sold for more than market value.

When you find sellers exaggerating or telling you something that you learn is not true, gently point it out. Becoming confrontational or argumentative does not move you closer to a deal.

If you let it slip that you have learned the truth, the sellers may feel that they have to compensate in some way. For example, if they misstate the price of another house that has sold in the neighborhood, print out a list of all of the properties that have sold. On your next meeting, show them the list without comment. Let them respond.

The other reason to ask questions is to test the sellers and measure their level of interest in doing business with you. People, especially people under stress, are looking for someone they trust with whom to do business.

What is the first thing that you notice about someone trying to sell something of value like a car or a property to you? If that person acts evasively, or seems slick to you, how do you react? I hope you thought "this person makes me nervous and guarded," not "I can outsmart him." It's hard to outsmart a con artist, because he plays by a different set of rules. He will lie to you and cheat you without remorse.

You want to only do business with people who you think you can trust. Then check everything they tell you to make sure that they are truthful.

Here are a few questions that will tell you a lot about the owners' situation and let you know if you are building trust. Notice that the first questions are easy to answer; the questions then get progressively more difficult. Owners who are not ready to sell, or who are not comfortable with you, will refuse to answer the harder questions. Sellers who have realized that they need to sell and who are ready to do business with you will answer them all.

1. Who are the owners of the property?
2. What is the legal description of the property, and how large is the lot? (ask to see the title insurance policy and survey if they have one to get this information)
3. How large is the house?
4. How old is the house?
5. Is there anything wrong with the house?
6. How long have the owners owned it?
7. What did they pay for it?

8. How much do they owe now?
9. Who is their lender(s)?
10. Who is their contact at the bank?
11. What is their interest rate and payment?
12. Are their payments current?
13. When did they make their last payment?
14. If they can't sell, what is their plan?

Other information you need before making an offer:

1. Your cash on hand and your ability to borrow.
2. The amount of monthly cash you are willing to invest if the house has a negative cash flow.
3. The value of the property, plus or minus 5 percent.
4. The general condition of the property. You can have it inspected after the offer is accepted, but you may want a contractor to look over any specific items like a roof, furnace, or air-conditioning unit before you make an offer. Offers that have you taking the property in "as-is" condition are easier for a seller to accept. Your offer can be as is subject to an inspection.
5. How much rent it will produce. Again, give yourself a plus or minus 5 percent range, and be conservative.

Making the Offer

After you have asked the above questions and have the information covered, you are ready to make an offer. Here is how you might think through a typical offer before you present it to the seller.

Case Study: Homeowner with Equity Needs to Sell Quickly

John and Mary own a house they purchased for $200,000. Today's retail value is about $400,000, and they owe $280,000 with payments of $2,500 a month, including taxes and insurance. In addition, they are three payments behind and owe $7,500, plus $500 in late fees or $8,000 as of this week. Their next payment is due in two weeks and their lender is anxious to work out something instead of foreclosing.

You think the house is worth $400,000, plus or minus 5 percent, or between $380,000 and $420,000 (rounded). The market rent is between $2,000 and $2,200 per month, so if you use the lower number for rent in your calculations, you figure the house will cost you about $500 a month to hold for the next five years. That assumes there will be a 5 percent rent increase a year. At a 5 percent increase a year, or $100 additional a month, the rents should cover the payments in about five years.

These round numbers are, at best, a guess. Taxes and insurance costs may rise, and there may be repairs needed. Unless the rental market is strong, you may also have some days during which the property is vacant. The offset is that the principal payment on a 30-year mortgage amortizing at 7 percent for a loan of this size is about $250 a month. The rents may increase each year (not just at the end of the five years), so this is a conservative projection.

To buy this house you need to be in a position to write a check to the lender for about $8,000; you also have to be willing to pay an additional $500 a month for 60 months, adding another $30,000. Rounded up, your total investment in this case would be about $40,000 over the next five years. At the end of the five-year period, the house should begin paying for itself and liquidate the remaining debt.

The question is, how much should you offer the sellers for their equity? Remember, they paid $200,000 and now owe $280,000. They have pulled out $80,000 in profit and are now unable to pay back the loan. If you offer to take the responsibility for their loan, make up their back payments of $8,000, pay next month's payment due, and give them $10,000 cash to move, your total price will be about $330,000. About $20,000 will be your cash invested today (for the down payment of about 5 percent of the property's current worth) and the other $30,000 is the cash-flow loss that the house will produce over the first five years. The balance of the price is their $280,000 loan, which you will assume.

Is a price of $330,000 (this includes the negative cash flow for the first five years) on a house worth at least $380,000 a good deal if you can buy it with $20,000 down? The answer depends on your market. If you can find a better deal, then this deal is not good enough. If you cannot find a better deal, then look at the results of this investment over about a 10-year period of time.

Ten Years Later

Let's assume that you then hold the house until it doubles in value. Again, to be conservative, we will assume in this example that the loan does not pay down, but in reality it will pay down significantly by the time the property has doubled.

You sell the house for $800,000, pay whatever tax is due at the time, and the difference between $800,000 and the $280,000 loan value is your profit. If the house took 10 years to double in price, you would have a gross profit of $520,000 on a total investment of $50,000. This does not count any profits that you might make from the rents after the first five years of making contributions, nor the loan amortization.

All of these numbers are best guesses, and you need to plug in your knowledge of your market. Some markets appreciate at higher rates, some at lower ones. In your town, some streets in some neighborhoods appreciate at higher rates than others.

If you buy a good house on a street in your town with better-than-average appreciation potential, then these numbers could be low. On the other hand, if you live in a town where it takes longer than 10 years for a house to double, you may consider selling it after 10 years anyway. Suppose it went up only half as much, to a price of $600,000. Would a $220,000 profit on a $50,000 investment over a 10-year period be a good investment for you?

Of course, this is before any income tax you might owe, but so is a profit from a stock or the interest on a savings account. The question is, where do you want to put your money for the next 10 years?

Make Your Offer to Both Owners at the Same Time

When two people own a house together, as they often do, always make your offer to both owners at the same time. If you present your offer to one person, even if she loves your offer, when she explains it to her partner, the response is predictable. Because the second owner was not involved in making the decision, he will have a hard time embracing it. The result will be a counteroffer to you.

While there is nothing wrong with a counteroffer (you may have started a little lower than you needed to, expecting a counteroffer), you can avoid the good guy–bad guy routine by having both sellers in the room when you make your offer. If they want to think it over, offer to leave them alone for 10 minutes to talk it over.

Preforeclosure

Do *not* let them take your offer with them and get back to you. Explain that you have two properties that you are close to buying, but you can only buy one. If they do not want your offer, you will make an offer on the other property. You want to give them the first chance, but if they reject your offer you want to be free to negotiate with the other sellers.

This is probably all true. While you may be willing to buy one good deal this week, you should not buy two, until you get the first one closed and rented. Buy one, rent one, and then start looking for the next good deal. Looking at two deals at the same time is good for you. It is twice as much work, but it allows you to make direct comparisons of two potential investments. Every house and every owner's situation will be different. You can compare the amount of money you will be required to put down with your monthly cash flow and your perceived discount off the real value of the house.

In the above case, you were able to buy this house.

House value	$380,000
Loan balance	$280,000
Cash at closing	$20,000
Cash flow first five years	($500) a month

Compare it to a similar house on the same street:

House value	$380,000
Loan balance	$200,000
Cash at closing	$60,000
Cash flow first five years	$0 a month (breaks even)

Unless you have the $60,000 down payment, you can only buy the first house (by yourself, that is—you could bring in an investor with the cash you need). But assuming that you had $60,000 today, which house would you make an offer on first? You can't buy them both. The first house is $80,000 below the market, and the second one is $120,000 below the market. The down payment on the first house is only $20,000 compared to the $60,000 on the second house. The second house has payments low enough that the rents will cover them. Both are good deals in a market with some upside potential over the next 10 years. If you are looking at both, you can continue to compare one to the other. While it is hard to tell if one house is a good deal, it's easier to tell which house is the better deal.

Helping a Seller Make a Good Decision

Sometimes sellers do not recognize the seriousness of their situation. If you suspect that this is the case, try asking the following questions.

1. Have you made arrangements to have your furniture stored or moved?
2. Do you know where you are moving to?
3. Do you have enough money for the rent and deposit?
4. Do you know the date that you have to move out?

Before you can help them, they must recognize that they have a problem. If they still think that someone is going to bail them out or pay them a lot for their property, they might wait until the day before the sale to accept an offer. The longer they wait and the closer the sale date is, the lower the offers will be. At some point, it will be too late to make a deal with the lender. The only way they will be able to stop a sale is to pay the lender all cash. An all-cash buyer will pay far less than a retail price.

Getting Them to Accept Your Offer or Make a Counteroffer

When you are with sellers whom you believe really need to sell their house and are in a position to make someone a good deal, you should buy that house. I have missed several good deals because I made an offer and then let them think about it. In every case, they sold to someone else who did not let them think about it. If someone is three payments behind on his or mortgage, that person needs to sell now while he or she still has something to sell.

There are several reasons that a homeowner may not accept your offer when you make it:

1. They may have another interested buyer who they hope will pay them more.
2. They may want to check with a family member or friend.
3. They may want to check with their lawyer.

Case Study: Lawyer and Friend as Negotiator

A couple who had lived in a house for many years had borrowed money on a private second home when the husband lost his job. He was not actively looking for a job, and their house was not on the market. The holder of the second was about to foreclose, but asked me if I wanted to buy the note instead. I agreed to buy it subject to talking to the owners. I set up a meeting with the owners and, after some conversation, I learned that they were also behind on the first, and were resigned to losing their home because employment chances were slim.

I offered to buy their house, solve the problem with both loans, and, rather than writing them a check for their equity, I would let them continue to live there for a nominal amount for six months. This would give them time to find employment and another place to live. They wanted to consult their attorney, so I asked them to call him. They arranged a meeting with their attorney, which we all attended. The attorney thought that I was not paying enough for the house. I said that they needed to sell immediately to avoid a foreclosure and offered him the house if he would pay them more and close right away. After a few minutes of thought, he said no, and we signed a contract and closed later that week.

Before You Make an Offer, Ask These Qualifying Questions

1. If I make you an offer today, are you ready to make a decision to sell?
2. Is there anyone else who you have to talk to before you make this decision?

If they do have someone else they need to talk to, set up a meeting right away and meet with that person and the sellers at the same time. Few sellers actually have an attorney, and most do not want to involve someone else in their financial affairs. By asking these questions before you make an offer, you can overcome these two roadblocks to making a deal.

Once you make an offer, you want them to negotiate with you right away. Stress that time is literally money to them. Every day they wait will reduce the amount that they can get for their house.

Caution: When people are in foreclosure, they are under stress. If they agree to sell today but later want out of a contract, it is in your best interest to let them out. If you hire an attorney and try to force them to sell, a judge may well rule against you, considering you to be a profiteer who buys a house from a distressed seller. Overreaching, or taking unconscionable advantage of a seller, often leads to a deal falling apart.

Getting Them to Sign the Contract

Make an offer that you think solves the current owners' most pressing problem. Often it will be money to move and to rent a new place to live. Sometimes it will be the money to move to another town for work. Occasionally, cash will be needed for the owners to pay some other expenses.

Get them to specifically identify what they need. Need is different than want. For example, I *want* a new jet. I *need* water, food, and shelter. Make sure you are dealing with their needs. Sellers sometimes price their property based on a want.

Write down your offer on paper and then explain how you will show them the things that are most important to them:

1. How you will deal with their loans
2. How much money they will get
3. When they will get it
4. When they have to move
5. What they have to do when they move

Present your offer with an explanation of the above and listen. Maybe there is something else that they need that you can provide them that you did not know about before. For example, maybe they need $1,000 to rent a truck to move their furniture to another town where they are moving in with their parents.

Solving Their Housing Problem

Perhaps the most pressing problem people losing their home have is where to live. If they lose a house at a foreclosure sale, they will receive no cash for their equity so they may not have enough cash for rent and a deposit on another house.

Some states, Georgia being notable, have enacted legislation requiring homeowners who sell to move out of their homes. The unintended consequence of such a law is that it penalizes the homeowners, not a buyer. Most states allow the seller of a home to lease it back. Research your state law before you agree to lease back a house to a seller. If your state law allows, you can rent them their home. This has several major advantages:

First, they don't have to go through the trouble of moving.

Second, they avoid the expense of moving, transferring utilities, and changing schools.

Third, a more subtle but important consideration, their neighbors, friends, and family may not know of their financial troubles, and they can eventually make a more orderly move to a new house or apartment.

How Can Someone Who Can't Make the House Payments Pay You Rent?

You have to be careful not to put homeowners in a rental situation where they will fail. If they cannot afford to make a $1,200-a-month house payment, then unless something has changed they will not be able to afford to pay you $1,200 a month in rent.

They may be able to pay a smaller amount and while paying the lower amount may be able to save up enough to move to another house that they can better afford. Before you offer to rent them their house back, ask them what they can afford in monthly payments. Make them calculate an amount based on their real income today, and the expenses that they have to pay. Luxuries like cell phones, cable TV, a newer car, and credit card account may have to be discarded in order to leave enough income to rent a decent place for their family to live.

For example, if two adults are working and their combined take-home pay is $4,000 a month, they should be able to pay about one third, or about $1,300 a month, in rent and live on the other $2,700 a month. If they have high car payments or credit card payments, then $2,700 may not cover their current expenses and they will have to come up with a plan to reduce those expenses until their income increases.

Many people buy luxuries like new furniture or a big-screen TV on great terms, like no payments until the following next year. When the next year comes along, they become overloaded with payments.

Using the $4,000 take-home pay and $1,300 they should be able to afford for rent, you could devise a rent schedule that they could afford and would allow you to buy the house and make a profit.

Case Study: Junior Executive Leaseback

A young couple with kids in school was trying to keep up with their friends and neighbors and had bought a nice home, financing the furniture and cars that went with it. They overloaded themselves with debt and refinanced some of their consumer debt with a second mortgage secured by their home.

The new loan was at a higher rate and had high upfront costs that the lender included into the amount of the loan. They were able to make the payments until the variable interest rate increased. At that time, they began to be behind in making payments and were in danger of losing their home. They could no longer refinance.

Fortunately, they had some equity in their home. I offered them the chance to use some of their equity to help them stay in their home. Their current payments were $1,600 a month and they could not afford them. After some discussion, they agreed that they could afford $1,200 a month, and because they had school-age children, they would like to stay in the house at least five years until the kids had graduated. I agreed to purchase their house for the loan balances, and bring the loans current. I then agreed to lease them their house back for five years on the following schedule:

	Rent	Loan payments	Monthly shortfall	Annual shortfall
Year one	$1,200	$1,600	($400)	($4,800)
Year two	$1,300	$1,600	($300)	($3,600)
Year three	$1,400	$1,600	($200)	($2,400)
Year four	$1,500	$1,600	($100)	($1,200)
Year five	$1,600	$1,600	$-0-	$-0-

Total additional cash investment needed $12,000

In addition to allowing them to use their equity for rent, I agreed to pay them an additional $10,000, which I would treat as a security deposit, returning it as long as they paid their rent on time and left me the house in good condition when they moved.

If they decided to move out early, I agreed that they could still have their security deposit if they left the house clean and in good repair and gave me a 30-day written notice of their intent to move. In the first several years of the agreement, they had rent that was a bargain. Should they move, I would be able to rent it to another tenant at a higher price.

The loan balance was approximately $150,000, and the house was worth between $200,000 and $220,000. My agreement to pay approximately $8,000 in back payments, plus my agreement to subsidize $12,000 in rent for five years, plus my agreement to pay them another $10,000 when they moved out brought my total purchase price to $180,000.

While they had other buyers willing to take over their payments and write them a small check for their equity, my offer allowed them to stay in their home and keep their kids in the same school. The value of this was "priceless."

Another way to help out owners in danger of losing a house is to find them another house to move into. You may own another house that is more affordable. If you have another empty house, you could make them the same type of offer. You could offer to let them rent your other house for below-market rent for a certain number of months. That would give them an affordable place to live and relieve them of their currently unaffordable loan payments.

Additionally, if you want to sell the house that you are offering them to rent, you could incorporate it in your offer to them, and give them an option to buy your other house. This would give them a chance to recover some of their equity.

Critical Elements of a Preforeclosure Offer

If you ever lease a house back to owners who are losing it because they cannot make the payments, you need to do the following:

1. Charge them a rent that they are sure they can afford
2. Give them enough time on the lease so that they can solve their problem, get a new job, and so on
3. Offer them a significant security deposit so that they have an incentive to move out and leave the house in good condition
4. Do *not* give them an option to buy the house back. If you agree that they can repurchase their house, it may be construed that you are making them a loan rather than buying their house. The amount of profit that you make could be treated as interest. If your state has a usury law, and the amount that you are charging is deemed to be usurious, then you may be subject to both civil and criminal penalties.

Case Study: Toys for Equity

A couple approached me about buying their house. They were several payments behind on their mortgage, but they still had some equity. They had refinanced the house for more than they had originally paid and spent the proceeds on expensive cars and clothes. Now, they owed money to several credit card companies and were in danger of losing everything. The lender was willing to let me begin making their loan payments without calling the loan due, so I knew I could buy the house without writing a big check.

The sellers told me they needed $20,000 cash to pay off all of their bills. I asked them to bring me the current statements of all of their bills. They brought them in, and the total that they owed came to only about $10,000. I had them contact their credit card companies and a local creditor, and they all agreed to begin accepting lower payments and reduce the interest rate if the homeowners would begin making regular payments. I agreed to pay them $400 a month for 50 months for the equity in their house with the understanding that they would use that money to pay down their consumer debt. They would get to keep all of their new toys, and have 50 months of no credit card payments.

Case Study: Divorced Owner Needs Less Expensive House

A recently divorced homeowner was several payments behind on his payments on a house that was both too large and too expensive for a single person to support. He wanted to downsize and salvage any equity he could.

I had another house available for rent that I was willing to sell using a lease option. I offered the homeowner the opportunity to move into this less expensive house and to give him $10,000 credit toward the purchase price if he purchased it within three years. In addition, I would rent him the house for $200 a month under the market rent.

His current house:	Value	$300,000–$330,000
	Loan	$220,000
	Payments	$2,200
My rental house:	Value	$180,000–$200,000
	Option price	$180,000
	Market rent	$1,200
	Discounted rent	$1,000
	Option credit	$10,000

I was able to acquire his house by making up his back payments and offering him a far more affordable house with the opportunity to buy the house at a bargain price, on terms that he could afford.

When Buying Preforeclosures, Focus on What the Seller Needs

My friend, Peter Fortunato, is a master at putting together deals. While most buyers talk about how much money the seller will get, Peter goes to the next step and asks what they will do with the money if he gives it to them. Money has no real value. You can't eat it, live in it, or drive it. The fact that someone else will trade you something of value for it gives it value.

Many buyers and sellers get hung up on how much money someone will pay the other for their property. Especially when you are dealing with people who have immediate needs, offer them what they need; don't offer money. Suggest a house to live in, a truck to move the furniture, a prepaid storage unit, or a plane ticket to the town where their parents live. These things solve immediate problems.

Improving the Seller's Credit

Any time you buy a house with a loan in default on it, by bringing the payments current, or even just starting to make payments, you are helping the seller's credit. If you help the seller avoid a foreclosure or make them an offer that allows them to make their payments on time, their credit will improve. If they are behind on their payments or have a foreclosure on their record, they will be forced to pay a high rate of interest whenever they borrow, that is, *if* they can borrow.

Finally, as long as the loan which they originally signed is in existence, it will show up on their credit report. If you are buying their house (or even leasing it) and they have a contract that shows that you have the obligation to make the payments, they can use that to help them qualify for another loan. If you are making their payments on time, their credit will be improved. Even though they still have some liability, you have the responsibility for making the payments, so it will help them show enough income to qualify for more credit.

Whenever you agree to make a payment for someone, make sure that you have the cash on hand to make it. Don't rely on the property jumping up in value or on someone else paying you a quick profit. Either have the cash on hand or know that you can rent the property for enough to make the payments.

There are criminal penalties for promising to make someone's payments and then intentionally not making the payments. Always have a "Plan A" and "Plan B" when borrowing money. Plan A may be to rent, and if Plan A falls through, Plan B may be to sell part interest to an investor who has agreed to buy. A partial sale would dilute your profits but give you only half a payment to make and some cash to make it.

Top Ten Sources of Pre-Foreclosures

1. Walking through neighborhoods and talking with neighbors
2. Noticing houses that are occupied, but need repairs
3. Vacant houses—especially ones with out-of-town owners
4. Local lenders and small loan companies who will not lend a homeowner behind on their payment any more money
5. Realtors—who list property and know their owner's motivation
6. Bird dogs—those whom you would pay a finder's fee for a lead
7. Attorney, accountant, and clergy referrals
8. Workmen, contractors, suppliers who are owed money by the homeowner and want to be paid
9. Relatives or friends who want to help them keep their home
10. Investors who run "I buy houses" ads

7

The Most Exciting (Riskiest) Time to Buy: At the Foreclosure Sale

There are many reasons that properties sell at deep discounts at forced foreclosure sales. Although it's easy to get excited about the prospects of buying a property at a 40 to 50 percent discount, you need to understand the risks involved before attempting to buy at a sale.

Eight Reasons That You Need to Buy at a Deep Discount

1. *You often cannot get access to the property.* Owners losing a home in foreclosure will not be holding an open house for potential bidders at the sale where they are losing their house. Unlike buying a

preforeclosure, where you have the time to spend with the sellers and try to solve their problem, owners losing their house know they will get nothing from the sale. Often, dozens of potential buyers have already approached them, so they are wary of anyone calling or knocking at their door. Sometimes the property is rented. The tenants have no obligation to show you the property and are displeased that they soon will have to move. The risk to you as a buyer is that you will not have a chance to inspect the property so you will not know of its actual condition. It may have serious defects that you will not know of until you take possession. Even if the house is in good condition today and the sale is tomorrow, much can happen in 24 hours. The house could burn down, leaving only a lot. If the residents leave mad, they may take all that they can with them and give everything else away. Some houses in foreclosure are completely stripped, meaning everything that can be removed from the house is. That includes plumbing and wiring fixtures and even the pipes and wires.

2. *Even after the sale, the owners or others may be in control of the property.* The sale itself does not give you, as the buyer, legal possession of the property. You may have to evict anyone who is on the property. Typically an eviction after a foreclosure action is an abbreviated eviction, meaning it will take only a few days, rather than a normal eviction, which could take a month or more. However, as we just stated above, a lot can happen in a few days.

When I buy at a foreclosure sale, I make every effort to contact whomever is in possession of the property. It may not be the owners or tenants. It may be friends or relatives or just some people who saw an abandoned house and moved in. I offer them a flat amount, typically $500, if they will agree to move out, take their stuff with them, and leave it reasonably clean. If the house is in good condition, you may offer more. I would certainly pay an extra $1,000 to get the house in good condition rather than risk getting it back trashed.

3. *Current occupants of the house probably will not paint and clean on their way out.* Unless you can make a deal with them, you will probably get a house back that needs a lot of cleaning and repairs. Unfortunately, when people lose their home, they sometimes take out their anger on the house. Although this action violates both their contract with their lender and perhaps vandalism laws, you will not be able to collect any damages against someone who is too broke to make their mortgage payments. You just have to build into your bid enough to compensate you for any probable damage.

4. *It takes a skilled legal expert to know if the sale was properly conducted.* For a foreclosure action to wipe out all claims against the property, everyone who has an interest or a claim must be given proper notice so that he has an opportunity to protect his interest. This includes any party who may own part of the property or a tenant who has a lease on the property or any lien holder. If there is a second mortgage (or any junior or inferior lien, meaning behind the lien that is foreclosing) or trust deed, or if there is a lien against the property for work performed or perhaps unpaid taxes, then these lien holders must receive notice. This requirement protects all creditors, as it gives them a chance to bring current the loan that is foreclosing and protect their interest.

Sometimes mistakes are made by the clerk or trustee in charge of the foreclosure. One common mistake is either not sending the notice to all lien holders or not sending the notice to the correct address so that they actually receive it. Unless lien holders actually receive notice that their interest in this property is about to be wiped out, then they will still have an interest in the property after the sale.

5. *You may not get a clear title.* Sometimes a junior lien holder is not named in the foreclosure action intentionally. When this happens, that party's interest is not extinguished by the sale. For example, assume that there are two mortgages on a house and the first forecloses but the second is not named in the foreclosure action. At the sale these are the facts:

First mortgage amount	$100,000
Second mortgage amount	$50,000
House retail value	$200,000
Winning bid at the foreclosure auction	$100,000

At the auction, the high bid of $100,000 purchases the property and the first mortgage is extinguished and the mortgage holder receives $100,000. However, the second mortgage will not have been extinguished. It is now a first mortgage, as it is first in line to get paid. The buyer has acquired a house for $100,000 cash plus the mortgage of $50,000, which is now very well secured.

6. *The judge or trustee makes no warrantees as to the condition of the property or the title.* When you buy at trustee's sales or a judicial foreclosure, you will receive either a trustee's deed or certificate of title. Neither document contains any warrantees or guarantees about the condition of the title.

7. When buying at foreclosure, you do not have recourse against the seller if they do not give you good title; when you buy at a normal purchase, you do. For example, in a normal purchase, if you buy a

house and someone makes a claim against the title after you close, then you can ask the seller to extinguish that claim, which will typically require her to write a check to whomever has the claim. In addition to this recourse against the seller, who "warrants" that she has good title and is transferring good title to you, you can buy a title insurance policy. This policy insures your good title, and will pay to extinguish any claims against it.

8. *The terms of a sale are all cash.* Typically, when buying at foreclosure you can pay the amount you bid with a cashier's check instead of bringing a stack of hundred-dollar bills. A big disadvantage for a beginning investor is that at an auction you don't have time to borrow any part of your purchase price. At some auctions, you are allowed to make a deposit and pay the balance by 5 p.m. the day of the sale, or the next day. This requirement for an all-cash purchase eliminates the possibility of borrowing through normal banking channels, as you simply don't have time to have the property appraised and inspected and to close a loan before the end of the day.

9. *If there is a problem with the sale, your money may be at risk or it may take you a long time to get it back.* When you bid and win, then pay the auctioneer with a cashier's check, the auctioneer will negotiate the check and start the process of giving you title to the property. This process can take several days or, in some states, up to a week or more. Occasionally, something happens where the high bidder will not be awarded title. If the owner is able to raise the money to pay off his loans, he can redeem the property. When this happens, the high bidder will eventually receive back the money she paid for the property, but the process may take weeks and there will be no interest paid on the money.

If You Are Going to Bid

To learn about the local customs and to get a feel for how the bidding goes, attend several sales at which you are not going to buy. You will be less intimidated by the process if you understand it. Every auction is a little different. Each state, and even each county, has its own procedures.

When you don't understand why something has happened, ask a lot of questions. The people conducting the auction are paid to be there and are obligated to help you. Their charge is to conduct a fair auction and to get the best price for the property. Don't let other bidders intimidate you or discourage your questions. Ask and learn.

Before attending an auction where you plan to bid, attend several auctions and see if you can notice a difference in the way different people bid. Like poker players, some bidders will be very aggressive in the beginning to scare others away. Some will bid the minimum amount over nearly every bid, hoping to convince the opposition that they are determined to get the property. Others will lay back and watch everyone else bid, making only one bid right at the end.

The competition at the sale may be experienced and well funded. Some bidders attend nearly all of the sales and know each other. Although it is not legal, they may even take turns bidding so that one does not run up the price for the other.

Before You Bid

Be prepared! You need to know the following information or do the following things before you make a bid on property being sold at foreclosure:

1. *Know what the house is worth and how much money it will probably need in repairs.* Estimate high.

The Most Exciting (Riskiest) Time to Buy

2. *Always establish the highest price you are willing to bid and write it down before you attend the sale.* Do not exceed this bid, regardless of the competition.

3. *Review or have your attorney review the file to ensure that you know exactly what you are bidding on and that other lien holders and owners have received proper notice.* Sometimes it's the holder of a second mortgage foreclosing.

4. *Have your cash lined up before you attend the sale.* Two good sources of cash to buy at foreclosure sales are bank lines of credit and loans from investors. These loans can be unsecured or secured by another asset or property. After you buy a property at a foreclosure, you probably will want to make repairs and maybe rent it before refinancing it to repay a line of credit you used to buy the property.

5. *If appropriate, contact anyone in residence to make him an offer to pay him to leave the house in good condition when you buy it.*

6. *Plan to go to the house immediately after the sale.* If you have previously contacted the residents, now you can confirm your agreement if they will agree to move out peacefully. As you will not have legal possession, be cautious. Whomever is in possession may not be friendly, and you do not want a confrontation. Try to talk to whomever is living there, and offer to pay them if they leave it in good condition. Make notes or take pictures, if possible, of the property showing its current condition.

7. *Although they are unlikely to have any assets, they may recognize you as someone who knows what she is doing, and this may help them to do the right thing.*

8. *If you are not the winning bidder, introduce yourself to the winner, and ask if he would be interested in selling.* He may be willing to take a small, quick profit.

9. *Sometimes a lender will actually attend the sale as well as send an attorney or representative; look for nonbidders who are interested in the results and introduce yourself as a buyer of REO (bank-owned) properties.* You may locate a source of other opportunities.

8

The Safest Time to Buy: After the Sale

Most investors are conservative by nature. Speculators have the good stories. Investors have the money. A safe, conservative time to buy a property is after the lender has taken title after a foreclosure sale. It is safer for several reasons:

1. *You have a chance to do a thorough inspection of the property after it is vacated.* Before a sale, you might get a quick tour of a house, but after a sale, you and a good inspector can spend hours in the house. Even more important, when the house is empty, you eliminate the risk that the owner will damage the house while

leaving. If the house is damaged before you close, the seller bears the risk of that damage.

2. *Rather than writing a large check to buy at the sale, you can seek out a lender, which will finance your purchase.* If there is something seriously wrong with the property or the condition of its title, it will be exposed as the property and its title are examined during the process of obtaining a new loan.

3. *You can arrange for financing prior to your purchase.* This gives you a chance to shop rates and terms and borrow on the best available terms. Don't overlook asking the lenders or sellers to finance for you. If they are willing to finance 80 percent of the price at a good rate, then you could afford to pay a higher rate for the top 20 percent or bring in a partner. Having time to shop financing gives you the opportunity to negotiate the lowest possible payments. Lower payments make the deal safer.

4. *You can get a title insurance policy insuring your interest and the interest of your lender.* Perhaps the biggest risk in buying foreclosures is the chance of not getting clear title to the property on which you are bidding. An undisclosed lien or interest in the property could cost tens or hundreds of thousands of dollars to buy out.

5. *You can take your time negotiating the deal.* You have no deadlines pressing you like a pending foreclosure. This allows you to compare this property with other potential investments. You can carefully prepare your strategy and your offer. When you are buying, never be in a hurry. Look for a seller in a hurry and then slow things down. The lower your offer, the safer and more liquid you are. If you decide that this is not the house for you, if you bought it cheap enough, you should be able to make someone else a good deal and still sell it quickly for a profit.

At the Sale, There Will Be One of Several Potential Outcomes

1. *The sale may be postponed or rescheduled.* A large number of sales are rescheduled. Often a mistake is discovered in the process and the foreclosing trustee or clerk must file an amended notice of sale. Occasionally, a seller will be able to talk a lender into postponing a sale with the promise of a payoff from a pending refinance or sale. If a lender thinks that she will get all of her money, she would rather wait than take a chance on a sale that would bring in only part of his or her money.

2. *The sale will take place and the lender will end up with the property.* All lenders hope that a foreclosure sale will allow them to recover their capital invested. Acquiring a property through foreclosure is the last thing that a lender wants. When this happens the lender no longer has the protection afforded to lenders. They are now property owners and have liability and all the cost of maintaining an empty house. The house may need work. They owe attorney's or trustee's fees for the foreclosure. They will probably list the property with a broker and then have to pay a commission. All of these costs are a drain on the lender.

   Some lenders will have thousands of foreclosures. Their cash flow will have a dramatic reversal. The more foreclosures a lender owns, the better the deal you will be able to make. Just be sure to buy a property that you want to own.

3. *The sale will take place and another bidder will acquire the property.* The other bidder could be a user but is more likely an investor hoping to make a profit. Always approach the winning bidder at a sale, even if you don't want to buy the property that he bought. Maybe he owns another property that you would want to

69

own, or maybe he has a lot more cash and would loan you money to buy a property.

After the Sale, There Are More Opportunities

1. *If the lender gets the property, it will want to sell it.* A lender would like to recover its capital but routinely sells for less than the amount that it has invested. Lenders are keenly aware of the cost of owning and maintaining an empty property.

   There are two reasons that you should make very low offers to lenders. First, you will never hurt a banker's feelings. The bank has no personal attachment to this property.

   Give the bank a chance to trade its empty house which costs it money every day to own for your cash which it can lend out for a profit or use to make payroll.

   The second reason that a lender will make you a great deal is that it's not the bank's money. Yes, bankers work for the stock-holders and it is the stockholders' money, but the banker on the phone selling you this property is much more interested in getting rid of a house than getting the money back. The house is a daily pain in the neck, and it negatively affects the bank's cash flow.

2. *If another investor buys the property, she may want to sell it.* When you make an offer to the investor, you have many choices in what you can ask the investor to do for you. If you are willing to buy from her at a higher price, ask for some terms that will allow you to buy without going to a bank and getting a new loan.

Case Study: Buying from an Investor After the Sale

Ivan bought the house at the foreclosure sale for $150,000 cash. He thought he could sell it for about $225,000 to a user after doing a minor amount of work to it. Investor Tom offered Ivan a quick sale with a 10-day closing at a price of $180,000 in as-is condition, if Ivan would take a $25,000 down payment and hold a note for $155,000 payable at 8 percent interest only for five years. Ivan accepted and calculated that he would be receiving 8 percent of $155,000, or $12,400 a year, in income on his $125,000 remaining investment. (This was his original $150,000 investment less the $25,000 down payment Tom paid him at the closing.) He would also receive $25,000 in additional profit in five years. This return would be secured by a first mortgage, and if Tom defaulted, Ivan would happily take the property back. His well-secured investment would require no work on his part. It would free him up to buy another foreclosure. Ivan had a considerable amount of money in the bank that was earning 4 percent, so the nearly 10 percent interest he earned on this deal (not counting his profit) was attractive to him.

Rights of Redemption

In most states, a homeowner can pay off his loans and redeem his property up until the moment of the foreclosure sale. In some states, a homeowner can redeem his property after the sale within a specified period of time. The redemption period can run from a few days to up to a year and varies from state to state. Research and know your state law on redemptions.

Building Wealth Buying Foreclosures

While few homeowners actually redeem their property after losing it in a foreclosure sale, the fact that they can do so opens a window of opportunity. If they can redeem their house, they can then sell it to you. To redeem a property, the homeowner typically must pay off the loans that were foreclosed plus pay any costs incurred during the sale. This amount varies from state to state. If the loan balances that were foreclosed were considerably below the market value of the property, then there is an opportunity.

Case Study: House Redeemed

Sellers walked into my office and announced that they had just lost their house in foreclosure and asked if there was any way to get it back. After some questioning, I learned that the house sold for $100,000 and was worth more than $180,000. The outstanding loan balances were only $95,000, so even though the house sold for more than the loan balances, the owner could redeem it for the amount of the loans due plus the cost of the sale.

I agreed to buy it from the seller and pay them $10,000 cash at the closing (in three days) plus I would write a check directly to the court for the amount necessary to redeem the house. They agreed, as without me they would receive nothing from the sale. I had an attorney prepare the necessary documents to transfer title to me. As I was purchasing from the owner, not at the foreclosure sale, I could obtain title insurance. The bidders who thought that they had bought the house at the foreclosure were surprised to learn that they had not bought the house. It took them several weeks to recover their all-cash bid.

Buying for Less Than the First Mortgage Balance at the Foreclosure Sale

The foreclosing lender does not always bid the entire amount due them at a foreclosure sale. When money is tight and lenders are trying to raise cash, they sometimes decide to accept a low bid at a sale rather than taking title to another house.

Whenever you see a house that you want to buy going to foreclosure, research it and be prepared to bid, even if the amount owed to the lender is far higher than you are willing to pay. Then if you attend the foreclosure sale and the lender bids in a lower amount, you might be the only bidder prepared to bid and can buy a bargain.

Case Study: Always Be Prepared

One lender had a $300,000 first mortgage that it was foreclosing. The market was soft, and the retail value of the house was between $250,000 and $275,000. The lender bid only $175,000 and an investor who had researched the property and wanted to buy the house was prepared to bid, and acquired the property for $175,500.

Choosing Your Strategy

Warren Buffett's first rule of investing is "don't lose money." His second rule is "don't forget rule number one."

It is far better to pass up a potential profit than to lose most of your capital on one bad deal. Don't look for excitement by taking financial risks. If you need excitement in your life, take up sky diving or learn to fly. When you invest, it should be as close to a sure thing as possible.

Your approach to buying foreclosures is likely to mirror your personality. If you are conservative, buying after the sale will fit you well. If you are more of a risk taker, know that although buying after the sale is less exciting, it can be as profitable as you can buy more properties with the same amount of cash. Buying at sales consumes loads of cash, whereas buying after gives you the ability to buy with a small down payment.

9

The Most Profitable Time to Buy: Buying the Note(s) Before the Sale

A well-kept secret among experienced foreclosure buyers is the opportunity to buy a promissory note secured by a house before a foreclosure sale. Lenders who have filed a foreclosure are facing the distinct possibility of taking a large loss on the loan involved. Most lenders are investors, not speculators. Given the choice between a sure thing and a chance of more money later, most will take the sure thing today.

This is not a short sale (see Chapter 10) where the lender actually satisfies the note and mortgage. This is buying the mortgage and note and having it assigned to you. Although short sales and foreclosures are more common, actually purchasing a mortgage and note from a lender has significant advantages and can be extremely profitable for the buyer. An advantage to the lender is instant gratification. Rather than wait for a foreclosure or for a buyer to make a short sale offer, it can sell its note and get a check this week. Another advantage to the lender is that it knows exactly how much it will receive. A foreclosure sale could bring more or far less. A short-sale offer is typically a low offer and many never close. On the buyer's side, you are not bidding against another buyer at a foreclosure sale. You are the only buyer, and if you find the right lender, you can make a great deal.

Unless the lender is in your town, most of the conversation and negotiation with the lender will take place on the phone. Lenders commonly do business over long distances on the phone. Although it may seem unusual, thousands of loans are sold every day by lenders. You will typically be buying a loan where the borrower is in trouble. This is a loan the lender would like to sell.

Case Study: Out-of-Town Lender Wants Out Now

In a neighborhood of well-maintained custom houses sat an empty four-bedroom house with a pool, built on two golf course lots. The house was owned by a couple who divorced and then individually filed bankruptcy. After the couple abandoned the house, it was vandalized, and at that point in time the house needed a considerable amount of work.

The loan balance, due to an out-of-state lender, was approximately $200,000. I made a list of the repairs the house needed and took a number of pictures. I sent the lender my assessment and photos along with an offer of $90,000 for the mortgage.

The lender sat on my offer and then counteroffered at $98,000. I reinspected the house, found even more damage, and lowered my offer to $85,000. (An important legal point: When you make an offer and the other party counteroffers, their counteroffer releases you of any obligation on your first offer. When the bankers counteroffered at $98,000, they could not change their mind and accept my original $90,000 offer unless I agreed to it.)

The bankers took only a day to respond with another counteroffer of $92,000. I countered back at $88,000 and bought their mortgage at that price.

At this point, I owned a $200,000 mortgage secured by a house worth between $170,000 and $180,000. It needed about $20,000 worth of repairs, and with the repairs would again be worth about $200,000. I contacted both owners and negotiated to buy each of them out for $1,000 cash. They signed a deed and I was able to buy title insurance. I now owned a house that needed work with a total investment of about $90,000.

Rather than making the repairs I agreed to sell it to one of my tenants who was looking for a larger house and did not mind taking on a project. The tenant and I agreed on a price below the retail price and I financed it for one year. In six months, he had made the repairs and was able to refinance it for enough to pay me off and put a little money in his pocket.

We nearly doubled our money in six months with a very low-risk deal. If the house had sold at a foreclosure auction, it would probably have sold for between $100,000 and $125,000. Buying the mortgage directly from the lender before the foreclosure sale eliminated all of our competition.

When a Property Has Two or More Loans

Many homeowners have more than one loan against their house. A lender with a second (or third) mortgage, junior to other loans, is in a position to lose the entire investment if the mortgage in front of them forecloses.

Recognizing that lenders have a potential for a large loss gives investors an advantage when they are buying a house.

Some investors are scared away by a house encumbered with several mortgages and miss the opportunity for large profits. When you find a house that you like and it has several loans or other liens against the property, there may be an opportunity to buy those loans for large discounts.

Case Study: Worried Lender Wants Cash Today

A lender made a second mortgage loan behind a first. The balance on the first mortgage was $120,000, and the balance on the second was $90,000. In a falling market, the house had dropped in value from $260,000 to $210,000. A foreclosure sale could possibly bring only the balance on the first mortgage, leaving nothing for the holder of the second.

The holder of the first mortgage began foreclosing. The lender in the second position had the right to write a check to bring the payments on the first current or to pay off the first to protect this investment. That would require investing more cash in a situation that now looked like a bad deal.

A buyer approached the lender that owned the second and negotiated to purchase the $90,000 second mortgage for a price of $30,000, subject to being able to negotiate a deal with the holder of the first. He then approached the lender that held the first mortgage who agreed to reinstate the loan and add the back payments to the amount of its loan.

The buyer closed on the purchase of the second note and mortgage, and then of the house. He then sold the house on a one-year lease option for a price of $199,000, with $5,000 down and payments large enough to repay the first. At the end of the year, the buyer had made a $49,000 profit on his $30,000 investment.

First mortgage assumed	$120,000
Cash paid for second mortgage	$30,000
Total paid for house	$150,000
House sold for	$199,000
Gross profit	$49,000

Buying a Note without Buying the Property

You can profit from buying a note at a discount without ever buying the property. In the above case, the buyer of the mortgage at a discount and the buyer of the property could be two different people. The buyer of the note needs $30,000 cash, but the buyer of the property actually needs little or nothing down. An investor could buy the $90,000 note for $30,000 cash and then let a new buyer buy the house and take over both loans.

Value of the house	$210,000
First mortgage balance	$120,000
Second mortgage balance	$90,000
Purchase price	$210,000

If you could buy the second for $30,000 cash, you would be in a position to allow new buyers to purchase the house subject to your loan. If they would buy the house, they would then be responsible for making the payments on both loans.

The homeowner would receive no cash from the sale but relief from both loans. Instead of having a foreclosure on her record, she would now have another owner making payments on time. The homeowner's credit would then improve. If the homeowner does not sell the house, as the owner of the second mortgage you would be able to foreclose and get title.

Case Study: A Note Buyer Helps the Homeowner Buy a House

A homeowner was behind on both his first and second loan payments. He had lost his job and planned on moving back in with his parents. Rather than allow him to have the loans foreclose, I agreed to help him find a buyer for his house if I could negotiate a deal with the lenders.

House value	$300,000
First loan balance	$150,000
Second loan balance	$100,000

The first mortgage was in foreclosure, and the sale was scheduled in a few weeks. Initially, I contacted the lender who owned the second mortgage and offered $25,000 for their loan. They agreed, concerned that they would receive even less at a foreclosure sale.

Then I approached the lender with the first mortgage and explained that I now owned the second and offered to bring the payments current if the lender would stop the foreclosure. The lender agreed, and I wrote a check for about $10,000 to bring the payments current. Now I had $35,000 invested. Because I had advanced money to make payments on the first, I could then add that amount to what was owed on the second. The balance on the second was now $100,000 plus the $10,000 advanced, for a total of $110,000.

I offered to sell the house to anyone who had enough income to make the payments on the first, and who agreed to begin making payments of $400 a month on the second, with the balance accruing interest for five years. At that time they would agree to refinance the house and pay off my loan. The $400 a month, or $4,800 a year, would give me better than a 13 percent return on my investment until the property was sold. At that time I would receive an additional $110,000 plus accrued interest on the original $35,000 investment.

There are significant differences between buying a note at a discount and a short sale. When lenders consider a short sale, they are adamant that the property owner receive nothing from the sale. In addition, with a short sale the seller may have a significant tax to pay.

Case Study: Short Sale Would Result in Huge Tax Liability

A seller approached me about a property that he had owned for years but had refinanced. He now owed about $500,000 on a property he originally purchased for less than $50,000. His loan was in foreclosure. If he lost the property in foreclosure, he would owe taxes on the $450,000 "profit" he made, as he owed $450,000 more than he paid for the property. This debt relief is taxed like a profit.

Even if this owner could negotiate a short sale for $350,000 where the bank would agree to accept $350,000 as full payment for the $500,000 debt, the owner would still owe the tax.

The solution to this problem was to buy the note from the bank for $350,000 and then renegotiate the payments with the owner to allow him to pay me the full $500,000 plus interest when he was able to sell the property. To secure my potential profit, he pledged two other properties with about $250,000 in equity as collateral. If the original property did not sell for enough to repay the full $500,000 plus interest, then he would pay me that balance when he sold the other properties. He could then look for an opportunity to make a tax-deferred exchange into a property that he planned to hold for a long time. His tax liability would not disappear, but he could postpone it indefinitely.

Buying from Private Lenders

Private parties, not banks, hold many second and third mortgages and most liens and judgments. Individuals and small businesses are very willing to take a significant discount on liens where they do not think they have a good chance of collecting.

Case Study: Unpaid Attorney's Fees

A seller of a house was in foreclosure. He had a first mortgage in default and owed a number of other creditors, including an attorney who had recorded a judgment against the property. The amount of the judgment was $25,000. When I offered the attorney $3,000 for his $25,000 balance, he agreed immediately and offered to come to my office and pick up the check. Apparently, he has lost confidence that he would ever be paid. I had him assign his judgment, not satisfy it. I was now in his place behind the first mortgage.

Value of the house	$175,000
First mortgage balance	$100,000
Judgment amount	$25,000

I bid at the sale, hoping to acquire the property for the $100,000 loan balance, plus my $3,000 investment in the judgment. Another bidder also wanted the house and bid against me. My highest bid was $125,000, which was the combined amount of the first mortgage and the balance on the judgment. The other bidder bid $126,000, and I let him have the house.

When the money was distributed from the sale, the first mortgage holder received $100,000 and I received $25,000 as the owner of the recorded judgment lien. I decided to take a quick small profit rather than write a check for $100,000 more to buy the house.

Seller Financing

Sellers sometimes finance all or part of the purchase price when they sell a house. Often the buyer will get a new first mortgage for about 80 percent of the purchase price and the seller will carry back a 10 percent second after receiving a 10 percent down payment. The transaction would look like this:

Value of the house	$200,000
Down payment	$20,000
First mortgage	$160,000
Seller carryback	$20,000

This arrangement helps a buyer with less income qualify for a loan, and an 80 percent loan will not be required to carry mortgage insurance; this further reduces the monthly payments. It also helps a property sell in a slow market.

The downside is that it creates a very risky mortgage for the seller. If the buyer fails to make the payments on the new first mortgage, and it goes into default, the seller is in a bad position. She does have the right to make payments on the first mortgage or to pay off the first to protect her position in the second. Would you write a check for $180,000 to protect a $20,000 second? Would you even write monthly checks of about $1,500 to protect a $20,000 position? I would not, and most investors would not.This creates a situation where the second mortgage has very little value and can be purchased for a small percentage of its value. If the first mortgage is in default, the second has no value, but you may still be willing to pay a token amount, say $500, in the hope that either the owner will stop the foreclosure and eventually pay you off, or that the house might sell for enough to pay you back plus a profit.

Case Study: Seller Carryback Goes Bad

A seller had sold his house to an investor who was able to qualify for a 60 percent loan with payments that would be covered by the rent. The seller agreed to carry back a mortgage for an additional 30 percent and received a 10 percent down payment at the closing.

The Most Profitable Time to Buy

Value of the house	$250,000
Down payment	$25,000
First mortgage	$150,000
Seller carryback	$75,000

The seller carryback had no payments and no interest for five years. The seller was concerned by the falling real estate market and approached me to buy his note.

When the investor purchased this house, he was wise enough to buy the house on terms that would allow him to rent the house for a positive cash flow. Had he agreed to make payments on the second, the house would have cost him money each month to own.

The note was reasonably well secured and it was behind a good existing mortgage with a low interest rate. The low payments on the first mortgage made the second mortgage more valuable. However, the lack of payments on the second made it unattractive to most buyers. When the holder of the note approached me, I made her the following offer: For the $75,000 note due in about five years I would pay $20,000 cash today and another $25,000 if the note was paid when due. Unless I received a payoff in full of the note in four years or less, I would not owe the note seller the second $25,000.

My prospective profit was $35,000 on the $20,000 investment over a four-year period. Although this is not a guaranteed profit, I liked the house, and if the owner could not pay off the note in four years, I would be happy to own this house with my $20,000 investment plus the current low-interest-rate loan.

If there was a default on the first mortgage, I would have to foreclose to protect my investment. We hoped that in four years the house would be worth more and it could be sold or refinanced. Then we would be paid off on our note, pocket a $35,000 profit, and pay the seller the balance due him of $25,000.

Builder Carrybacks

Builders become creative in selling inventory in slow markets. Some just discount their prices and sell at or below their cost. Others offer sellers attractive terms.

One successful technique is to allow the buyer to acquire a house by qualifying for a new 80 percent loan and by carrying back a 15 percent second mortgage. This gets a buyer into a house with only a 5 percent down payment and allows the builder to sell more quickly.

When the homeowner sells or refinances, the builder will be paid off. However, should the homeowner get behind on his payments, the builder will not be interested in paying off the first mortgage or taking the house back. This presents you with an opportunity to buy a fairly new house at about a 15 percent discount and with a nominal down payment.

When you find a homeowner in default with a second payable to the builder, offer to buy the house subject to the existing first mortgage, subject to negotiating a deal with the builder acceptable to you. Next contact the lender with the first to see if it is willing to let you take over the loan. If the loan has a low fixed interest rate and will let you assume it with little or no fee, then agree to take it over if you can make a deal with the builder.

Now go to the builder and offer $1,000 for the $15,000 second. He has no interest in taking the house back with a large loan on it. He will receive nothing if the house is sold at a foreclosure sale, because it would not bring more than the loan balance at a cash auction. You may be willing to pay a little more, but you should be able to buy that note for a small fraction of its original value.

Look for opportunities to buy a note in default before you buy a house or before a foreclosure sale. Most buyers are not looking for these opportunities, so you will have little competition.

10

Short Sales: Buying When the Seller is Willing to Walk Away

A short sale is the sale of a property where the lender agrees to accept less than the full amount that is owed to it. This type of sale occurs frequently and happens often during a slow real estate market.

From the standpoint of lenders, a short sale shortcuts the foreclosure process. Rather than having to wait for properties to go through foreclosure and then sell, lenders are given an opportunity with short sales to receive a cash settlement quickly. It gets them their money sooner than a foreclosure would and with fewer out-of-pocket expenses and less risk.

When lenders foreclose, they have to write a check to an attorney or trustee; often they will pay someone to secure the property and even make repairs. In addition, while they own the properties, they have to pay the expenses of taxes and insurance. Plus they will have the obligations of ownership, including maintaining and taking responsibility for the properties before they are sold again. Liability is part of ownership; lenders would prefer to avoid the liability.

Typical Cost of Foreclosure to a Lender

Here's what a lender could typically be expected to spend for a foreclosure:

House value	$300,000
Loan balance	$240,000
Fees and cost to foreclose	$2,000
Interest lost over six months (before, during, and after the foreclosure)	$9,200
Cost of insurance and taxes	$3,000
Cost to repair and maintain	$3,000–$30,000+
Probable sales price	$250,000
Real estate commission to sell	$17,000
Total out-of-pocket cost	$34,200–$60,000
Probable net	$215,800–$190,000

This discount of between $35,000 and $60,000 of the loan balance represents a discount of between 15 and 25 percent of the loan balance. This is in a case where the loan balance is not greater than the market value.

These are estimates. In a very soft market, the net could be even lower. If the market is strengthening, the net may be a little higher, but the costs of foreclosing, maintaining, and selling still must be paid.

Do Not Use a Rule of Thumb When Discounting a Loan

A 15 to 30 percent discount may not be large enough to allow you to make a profit. In some cases, the loan balance is greater than the property value. When this is true, you need to discount the loan by a greater percentage to have a reasonable chance of making a profit. If the same $300,000 house had a loan balance of $340,000, and you were willing to pay no more than $200,000 for the house, you would need about a 40 percent discount to buy at the $200,000 price.

By understanding these costs, as the lenders do, you can calculate a short-sale offer before they foreclose that will give them an earlier payoff and save them these costs. The expense that is not included in the calculations above is the cost for in-house staff to monitor and manage these properties. This amount can be significant.

While lenders will rarely solicit a short-sale offer, they will gladly receive them. The bank does not own the house, so your offer is to the seller of the house, and subject to the bank accepting a short sale or short payoff. The bank will insist that the sellers prove that they do not have other assets they could use to pay this loan and that they will not benefit from this short sale. So, the sellers cannot receive any of the proceeds from the sale or lease the house back.

The lender will want a letter from the sellers stating why they cannot make the payments and stating that they will receive no benefit from the sale.

The Effect of a Short Sale on the Seller

When lenders accept a short-sale offer, they may not release the borrowers from the loss they are taking on the loan. The lenders may try to collect the difference between what you pay them on their loan and the total amount due. However, lenders rarely pursue homeowners who have lost their homes for a deficiency in the payoff.

Most sellers are so happy to have sold their house that this issue is not a big one. Most sellers in danger of losing their houses just want to get rid of the payments and the house.

If the borrowers have debt forgiveness as a result of a short sale, then they may owe taxes on that amount. Most homeowners who are behind on their payments are not worried about paying income taxes; they are worried about next month's payment that they cannot make.

A short sale will not be as damaging as a foreclosure on the previous homeowners' credit report, but it will show. The good news is that after two years lenders will again be willing to make them a loan. In the meantime, if the sellers find a house that they can buy using a lease option, they can begin building equity.

Challenges to the Buyer

The greatest obstacle in buying a house using a short sale is the amount of cash you need to close the deal. The terms of a short-sale payoff to a lender are all cash, and a lender will want its money soon—often in a week. Although you can ask for a longer time in which to pay a lender, typically one will not give you enough time to resell the house or to go out and get a new loan.

If you have a lender willing to make you a new loan and close quickly, you could use a new loan to pay off the old one. Even better, if you have an established line of credit with a bank, you could use that to pay off the short-sale loan and then take your time selling or refinancing.

The temptation a buyer must avoid is to give the sellers money for their house. You will be required to sign documents stating that the sellers did not receive any money from you in this transaction. If you do pay them, that transaction may be considered bank fraud. Bank fraud is a criminal charge and is very expensive to defend. Do not cross this line. (Federal regulations have been proposed that would allow sellers to receive some cash in a short sale. Changes in this area would make short sales more attractive to sellers.)

How to Buy Using a Short Sale

Real estate agents are often familiar with short sales. If you are buying a listed property, they will do the work to get the bank to accept your offer. If you have never made a short-sale offer before, using a knowledgeable agent to put together the short-sale package and submit it to the bank will increase your chance of success. Plus you will get the opportunity to watch and learn.

About half of the properties I buy are listed with agents. I try to go through the listing agent. When the listing agent sells a property that she listed, she often gets twice the commission. This really motivates the agent to help put a deal together.

When you are buying a short sale through an agent, the agent needs to be optimistic that the deal will work because she will have to do extra work to get it closed. Often agents are very motivated if they have a listing about to expire and the owner has not had any offers. Add to that a motivated owner who is out of money and you have the formula for a short-sale offer that should work.

Case Study: An Agent Solicits a Short-Sale Offer

An agent with a listing that was about to expire called me to see if I would be willing to submit an offer to buy the house for less than the owner currently owed. The house needed some cosmetic work, but it was the type of work that could be done in a week or less by a skilled craftsperson.

Building Wealth Buying Foreclosures

The owner was out of cash and was not going to make another payment. The market was slow, but the house was in a desirable neighborhood and would sell within a few months at a lower price. I offered 25 percent below the loan balance and agreed to close in one week. The lender accepted, and I closed.

Immediately after the closing, I placed a for-sale sign in the yard and began making the necessary repairs. A young couple called me who had been looking for a house in that neighborhood. They already owned a smaller house with a low-interest loan. They wanted to make an offer on this house, but they were afraid to do so until they sold theirs. On the other hand, they really liked my house and did not want it to get away.

I asked for the information on their current house and made them this offer. I would accept the equity in their current house as a down payment on my house, as long as they could qualify for a new loan on the house that they were buying.

My house	$220,000 retail
My purchase price	$140,000
Their house	$120,000 retail
Their loan	$80,000
Their equity	$40,000
Their offer	$220,000 purchase price
Equity as down payment	$40,000
Subject to getting new loan of	$180,000

They were able to qualify for a new loan, and I accepted their house as a down payment. I subsequently sold their house on a lease option to a first-time home buyer.

Putting Together a Short-Sale Package

A lender who discounts a loan wants to make sure that the seller is not benefiting from the lender's loss. The lender will require documentation showing that this is a fair offer in the current market and that the seller is not getting any benefit from the sale.

The most important document to the lender is the HUD 1 form. This form is a projected closing statement (or net sheet) that shows the sales price, along with all the expenses charged before the lender gets its money. You can download a HUD 1 form at the HUD Web site (www.hud.gov) in the Forms section.

Lenders are not pleased with offers where others are getting paid all of their money and the lender is taking a loss on the deal. If the HUD 1 form shows a full commission and other fees being deducted before the lender gets a reduced amount, the offer may not be accepted. If the HUD 1 information shows minimal costs to the lender and has the buyer paying the costs while the seller gets nothing from the sale, then the lender is more likely to accept the offer.

In addition to the HUD 1 form, here's what lenders also want to see:

1. Documentation for the borrowers that shows that they cannot make the payments and have no other assets that could be used to pay this debt. Lenders will require a financial statement that lists the sellers' assets and liabilities and two years of past tax returns. In addition, a handwritten letter from the owner that explains the reason for the hardship will sometimes help lenders agree to an offer.

2. A recent appraisal or broker's opinion of the value.

3. If there is work needed, a bid from a reputable firm that shows the cost of repairs.

4. On the buyer's side, lenders will ask for proof of funds. They want to know that a buyer has the money on hand to close the sale. If you offer to buy for $200,000, then you should show them an account with a balance of $200,000, or a commitment letter from a lender for the amount that you need.

When Short Sales Work Best

Buying a property using a short sale takes a lot of cash. Unless you have a lot of cash or the ability to borrow from a bank on a line of credit, you may not be able to close, even if the lender says yes.

Here's when a short sale works best:

1. *You plan to buy and then refinance to get your cash out of the property and then rent it for enough to repay the loan.* For example, you buy a house worth $260,000 for $200,000. After closing, you would borrow the $200,000 at 7 percent on a 30-year loan with payments of $1,330.60. You know that you can rent it for enough to pay these payments and the other costs of ownership. Or, you are willing to contribute enough each month to make the payments until the rents increase to a level where they will cover the payments.

2. *You plan on first buying and then selling to an investor to get your cash back, and then rent for enough to give you both a fair return.* For example, you could buy the same house worth $260,000 for $200,000 and then sell half interest to an investor. Find an investor with enough cash to buy an undivided interest for cash and to loan you enough money to buy the other half interest.

   You could agree to sell an investor one-half interest in the house for $100,000 if he or she would agree to loan you $100,000 at 6 percent interest which you would use to buy the other half of the house. Your agreement could include that you would agree to manage the property and repay him the $100,000 when you sell the property. The note and mortgage should have a term long enough for the property to double in value in your market.

House value	$260,000
Purchase price	$200,000
Sale of half to an investor at a discounted price	$100,000
Borrowing from the same investor to buy your half	$100,000

You would then own the house 50–50 and split all of the income and expenses 50–50. As your coinvestor would have no debt on his half, he would have cash flow each month from the rental income on his half. He would also have the income from the $100,000 he loaned you at 6 percent.

Six percent of $100,000 is $6,000 a year, or $500 a month in interest.

If you could rent the house for enough to pay the expenses of taxes, insurance, and maintenance and have $1,000 a month left, you would have enough income (your half would be $500 a month) to pay your loan. As rents increase, your income would increase.

This would be a good deal for you, as you would own half interest in an appreciating house, which you would buy below the market without any of your own cash. It would also be a good deal for the investor, as he would own a property at a great price that is giving him a good return—and you are doing all of the work!

If the investor would rather borrow all of the money to buy the house, he could place a $200,000 loan on the property. Then he would have nothing invested in the house but would be responsible for making the payments on the loan. You could join him on this loan, and you would each have to sign the security agreement, the security deed or mortgage, and note.

3. *You plan to buy and then sell to a user for a quick profit.* Be cautioned: Sometimes when it's easy to buy, it's hard to sell at anywhere near a retail price. We sell most of our houses with some type of owner financing. It allows a buyer without perfect credit to qualify to buy a house.

In a down market, lenders tighten their lending requirements. Although it's a good time to buy, fewer can qualify for new loans. You can sell when others cannot by offering terms to buyers who want to buy.

Buying using a short sale gives you the opportunity to thoroughly inspect the house and to negotiate carefully, typically without competition. It also allows you to buy at wholesale prices. The challenge is to raise the cash, as the bank that is taking a loss on their loan will not lend you the money. It is a low-risk strategy for purchasing wholesale deals.

11

The Insider's Scoop: Understanding the Lender's Perspective

As a lender, I have experience with lending and managing existing loans. As an active buyer of property with loans in default, I talk often with lending officers and loss mitigation officers.

Bank officers and employees are loaning other people's money and have a responsibility to both the depositors and stockholders. A loan officer at a bank has a responsibility to the stockholders at that bank to make good loans. When some inevitably fail, then the officer is responsible to get as much money back as he or she can.

With small banks or small lenders or individuals who loan their own money, the same person who makes the loans will be involved in collecting the money. In a larger bank, a different department, often called the "loss mitigation department," will handle the collection function.

Lenders take what they think is an acceptable risk when they loan money. Sometimes the market changes and loans that looked good last year look bad at the present time. Of course, more than just the market changes, and borrowers' lives may change, causing a good risk to become a bad risk. Even the best borrowers occasionally have overwhelming problems.

When a borrower cannot repay her loan, the lender will want to talk with her. Often a modification of the terms will allow a borrower to survive and repay the loan. In most cases, this is a better solution for the lender than a foreclosure, which requires more money to be invested in a bad loan with no guarantee of repayment.

Lending officers are often compensated based on loan production. This can lead them to make loans to marginal borrowers, which in turn results in some loans going bad. These same loan officers have a personal interest that goes beyond their responsibility to the bank. If they develop a reputation for making many bad loans, they will soon be looking for other work. For this reason, a loan officer will sometimes be the key to solving a problem. This is especially true in smaller banks.

Your First Contact

When I am interested in buying a property that has a loan in default, my first call to a lender will be to the officer who made the loan. He has a personal interest in a resolution. Although he may not have the authority to restructure the loan, he probably knows the person in the bank who does. If he goes to bat for you, it increases your chances of successfully renegotiating a loan.

Understand that before lenders will talk with you, they will want a letter signed by borrowers authorizing them to talk to you about the loan. Get this letter early in your discussion with the current owner and borrower.

After talking to the loan officer, I get the number for the loss mitigation officer. If I cannot locate the loan officer, I get her name and phone number from the borrower. Make sure that the loss mitigation officer has received the letter from the borrower that allows the officer to talk with you, and then call.

In my initial call, I tell the loss mitigation officer that it may be possible to avoid a foreclosure if the lender is willing to make some concessions.

Sometimes They Hold Them, Sometimes They Sell Them

Some lenders keep the loans they make in their portfolio; they are referred to as "portfolio lenders." Others sell their loans to other investors. Many of the lenders who sell their loans retain the rights to service those loans and collect a fee for collecting the payments each month and for dealing with loans that go bad.

Some loans are sold to institutional investors who assume the servicing responsibilities. These loans are the most challenging to renegotiate.

When a loan is sold to another investor, it is sold with conditions. If the loan is flawed because of inadequate oversight or fraud, then the investor can give the loan back to the originator and get his money back. If an aggressive lender has overlooked credit problems of the borrowers, or used unrealistic appraisals to justify loans, or, as in one local case, funded loans to a builder who was not actually building the houses, then this lender can be forced to take back those loans and must repay the investor.

These problems are more likely to occur in a hot real-estate market, where the volume of loans increases dramatically and many new loan officers are hired to make loans. In addition to bank loan officers, mortgage brokers make loans directly for investors. Independent mortgage brokers rarely have the financial ability to refund the money to an investor for loans that involve fraud.

Getting to Yes

You have little leverage when dealing with a lender. The only advantage you have over your competition is your professionalism and good manners. The bank officer on the other end of the phone or across the desk has a pretty tough job. She hands out more bad news than good news.

If you hope to make a deal with a loss mitigation officer, here are a few tips:

1. *Give the officer something to work with.* The officer will generally be presenting your offer to her superior who will make the decision. Make her look good by giving her information that she needs to sell the deal to the boss.

   For example, furnish her with comparable sales, along with current listings in the area that support your case. If the house needs work, instead of just listing the work it needs, include a bid from a licensed contractor.

   If you are asking the lender to lower the interest rate or change the payments, give a reason that she can sell to her superior. If the rents will only support a certain payment, then document the current rent with a copy of the lease, along with the tax and insurance bill.

2. *If you are asking to take over the loan, give the lender enough information about you so that she can check you out and see that your credit is solid.*

3. *Always be pleasant and easy to deal with.* You may get a no one day, and a call back a week later with a yes, if you have left the relationship in good shape. The lender's motivation to sell or renegotiate can change daily.

Gauging the Motivation of the Bank

If a bank is in trouble, the officers are more likely to make you a good deal. Each quarter, every bank files a Report of Condition and Income, containing hundreds of accounting items pertaining to its financial condition. The FDIC publishes these reports online. Other Web sites, like www.ml-implode.com, track lenders that are in trouble.

Before you make an offer to a bank, you may want to research its current condition. When you find one in trouble, be nice, but lower your offer a bit to test its interest in doing business.

When a bank gets in trouble, sometimes the government will liquidate the bank and sell the assets, paying off the depositors with the proceeds. This is the last resort for a bank, as the stockholders will receive nothing and any depositor with an account balance over the FDIC-insured limit will lose the uninsured amount.

The other option is for the troubled bank to sell to a healthy bank. When this happens, the troubled bank sells its assets, including its loans and deposits, to a healthy bank.

In both of these cases, the loans the troubled bank has in its portfolio, especially the nonperforming loans, are targets for a discounted purchase. When a new lender buys a nonperforming loan, it has less, sometimes *far* less, than the first bank invested in the loan. It may then be willing to sell at a bigger discount or renegotiate on great terms. Look for these opportunities in your town, and make low offers on these properties.

Just as some sellers are easier to buy from, some loss mitigation officers are more creative and more cooperative than others. When you find one who is easy to deal with, keep his name and number and ask for him the next time you are dealing with that lender. The relationship that you develop is worth a lot.

Ask for Help, Even When the Loan Is Current

A lender can restructure a loan even when it is current. Recently I met with a borrower and the loss mitigation officer from his bank. The borrower had communicated with the bank that he was having difficulty, and then he set up a meeting with the lender. After showing that the property was for sale at a price that was below the market, and showing that he could not afford to make any more payments, the borrower got the lender to agree to modify the loan.

The lender agreed to drop the interest rate by 3 percentage points and give the borrower six months to sell the property without the obligation to make payments. They agreed to the modifications, even though the loan payments were current.

Most borrowers wait until they are in arrears before they contact their lender. Don't do that. The example above shows that lenders often want to help solve the problem, if you give them the opportunity.

12

Sixteen Ways a Lender Can Help You Buy a House

In the last chapter you gained some insights as to why bankers make certain decisions. Every bank is different, every real estate market is unique, and every person who works at the bank has his or her own personality. And one of them may just be having a bad day. All of these factors will affect whether or not a lender accepts your offer.

Bank managers have regular meetings and issue instructions to their loss mitigation officers. If the bank's loan portfolio is performing well, the message may be: "Don't give anything away." On the other hand, if it has several nonperforming loans or owns several properties on which it has foreclosed, then the instructions might be: "Make the deal that you can."

Rather than drive yourself crazy trying to figure out exactly what the lender is thinking that day, it's a better strategy to ask him to do something for you and then study how he reacts.

Not all lenders are bankers. Many are individuals. They may be even more anxious than a banker to make a deal if they are depending on the income from the note. While a banker's portfolio may contain thousands of loans with only a 1 or 2 percent default rate, a private lender may have only one loan with a 100 percent default rate.

These potential alternatives to foreclosure apply to bankers and private lenders alike.

Getting to NO!

Lenders have a lot of options they can use short of foreclosing on a loan. When I talk with lenders, I state that I would like to save them the time and money that it takes to foreclose. I then proceed to ask if they would do one or more things on the following list. If they are quick to say yes, I will ask them to do more, and keep asking until I get a no. If I get a no to everything, I will give them my number and ask them to call me if they become interested in avoiding the foreclosure.

A foreclosure can be good for you as a potential buyer, but it is rarely good for the lender and never good for the borrower. Once a bank forecloses on a property, it will become more motivated with every passing day to make a deal.

Profitable Solutions Other than Foreclosure

Once lenders see you as a catalyst to stop the foreclosure, they will be more receptive. When possible, arrange a face-to-face meeting with the mitigation officer or originating loan officer. Often this get-together is not possible because you live in different cities, so you will have to make your offers over the phone.

Sixteen Ways a Lender Can Help You Buy a House

It is always a good strategy to let the mitigation officer do most of the talking, because she may make offers to you that you have not even considered. The following litany of possible offers is not every one the officer could make you, but it will help you prompt her.

This list is ordered with the smaller concessions at the start. Begin asking for the smaller things, and work your way down the list. The person you are talking with may have the authority to grant you some of these. By asking, you can learn how much authority that officer has to make decisions.

The first five concessions are ones lenders often make rather than foreclosing.

1. *They can forgo late fees.*

2. *They can forgo back interest.*

3. *They can forgo late payments.*

4. *They can forgo attorney's fees.*

5. *They can agree to add any or all of the above to the amount of the loan.* Although it's always better to get forgiveness than forbearance if a lender will agree to add to the amount of the loan money that is due today, the benefit to you is nearly the same if you plan on holding the house as a long-term investment. If you plan on selling the house right away, then hold out for actual forgiveness of as much as possible.

6. *They can agree to lend you more money to finish or repair the house.* Many houses that you will buy in preforeclosure will need more cash invested in them before you can sell or rent them. Ask the lender to advance you more money under the current loan. Some loans have a "future advances" clause, which allows the loan amount to be increased. If not, they could make you a second loan secured by this house, or make you a loan secured by another property that you own.

7. *They can agree to allow you to take title subject to the existing loan.* Taking subject to a loan is different than assuming a loan. When you take title subject to a loan or any other lien against a property, you are acknowledging that there is a lien on the property, but not taking the personal responsibility to pay the lien. If you do not make payments on a loan or pay off another claim against the property, you may lose the property and any equity that you have, but you would not be liable to pay the liens if the property was sold at a foreclosure sale. Obviously, you do not want to buy a property unless you are certain that you can make the payments, or you would just be setting yourself up for a loss.

You would want to take title to a house subject to the loans in a situation where you hope to renegotiate the existing debt. For example, suppose the house has a first mortgage and two other smaller encumbrances, a second mortgage and a worker's lien:

House value	$240,000
Balance on first mortgage	$160,000
Balance on second mortgage	$30,000
Balance on worker's lien	$20,000

You do not want to take the responsibility for paying off these debts. You are taking title to the house, stopping the foreclosure on the first mortgage, and hoping that you can negotiate a repayment schedule with the other lien holders that will allow you to make a significant profit.

When you take title subject to the loan, your name will not appear on the loan documents, and the original borrower will still receive notices and statements for the loan. Have the seller write a letter to the bank, telling the bank that you are now making the payments for the loan and asking the bank to send you the payment coupons and any notices regarding the loan. If the loan has escrows for taxes and insurance, the payments will change over the years, and you need to know the amount of the new payments.

This loan will stay on the seller's credit report until you pay it off. If you make the payments on time, it will improve his or her credit.

8. *The lenders can agree to allow you to assume the existing loan without making you qualify.* Typically, to assume a loan, you will be required to submit financial records, make an application to the lender stating your income and expenses, and often pay a fee to the lender. If your assumption is approved, the lender will require you to sign an assumption agreement, transfer the loan to your name, and often try to extract a fee from you for the privilege. Although your name is now on the loan, the original borrower will also remain liable on the loan, and it will show up on her credit report until the loan is paid in full.

The only reason to assume a loan is to lock in a great interest rate or good terms. If the loan has an attractive interest rate, or if the lender is willing to negotiate a lower rate with you, then assuming a loan to lock in these good terms is a good strategy. It prevents the lender from calling the loan due or raising your rate in the future.

When the lender likes you more than the original borrower, he will agree to shortcut this process and waive the fees. He can check your credit in a matter of minutes; if you are a good credit risk, he will want you to assume this loan.

9. *They can agree to allow you to sell the house to someone else with the existing loan in place.* For the bank to agree to this

concession, it must be anxious to get the loan reinstated (probably due to its financial position) and trust that you will sell to a buyer who will keep the loan current. You would want this concession on houses that you wanted to resell with the loan in place.

An alternative would be to get the bank to allow you to sell the house to another with owner financing, allowing you to continue to make the payments to the bank. This arrangement is called a "wraparound mortgage." With a wraparound mortgage, you would still be responsible for making the payments on the bank loan and would finance the new buyer. If the loan to the bank is at a low interest rate, or if you can get the bank to reduce it as part of your negotiation, then you can build in an interest rate spread that gives you a higher-than-normal return. For example:

House value	$300,000
Balance on first mortgage	$180,000 @ 6% payable, $1,000 per month
Balance on second mortgage wraparound	$200,000 @ 8% interest only payable at $1,333 per month

You, as the holder of this wraparound mortgage, would collect the $1,333 each month from the new buyer and pay the bank the first $1,000 a month, leaving $333 a month, or $3,960 a year, cash flow return on your $20,000 equity in the note. In addition the equity in your note would increase each month by about $100, as the wraparound is an interest-only note while the first mortgage is an amortizing loan and paying down $100 a month in the first month.

10. *They can agree to reduce the interest rate.* The interest rate will have a significant impact on your profit over time. Always ask for a rate reduction. A 1 percentage point reduction on a $100,000 loan saves you $83.33 a month for the life of the loan. Over 30 years that's $30,000. Even if you are going to sell the house quickly, the lower rate may make the house more attractive to someone else, if he can qualify to assume it. Of course, the low rate may make it more attractive to sell with a wraparound like in the previous example.

11. *They can agree to defer the payments.* Deferring payments may give you or the current seller some breathing room. A deferment increases the lender's risk, but if the lender thinks that it will lead to a sale, generally she will be agreeable. Negotiate a deferment without late fees or other penalties. Ask for longer than you need, but fight for the minimum time you need to either rehabilitate or rent the property or sell it. You can get the lender to agree to both defer the payments and then to add them to the loan balance so that you do not have to write a big check at the end of the deferment period.

12. *They can agree to renegotiate the payments on the loan.* Changing the payments due on a loan will change the term of the loan. In the event you need even a lower payment to be able to break even on a house, you could agree to a balloon clause in the loan. A balloon clause states that the entire balance will be due at a certain date in the future, regardless of the payments. Lower payments always work to your advantage, but give yourself enough time to resell or refinance if you agree to a balloon clause.

13. *They can agree to make you another loan.* When you are buying from a lender, don't forget that its business is lending money. If you own another property that you would like to refinance at a

good rate, ask the lender for the money as part of your deal. You may be able to refinance another property you own to get the money to buy or pay off the loan. If the new loan and you are rock solid, then don't be shy about asking for a great rate, or ask the lender for a discount on its existing loan.

Case Study: Refinance and Buy

Bank-owned house value	$250,000
Balance advanced on first mortgage	$150,000
Other house we owned	$350,000
New first mortgage from lender	$300,000 @ 6%, 30 years

At the time, other investors were paying 8 percent for a comparable loan. Our 2 percentage point savings amounted to an interest savings of $500 a month, or $6,000 a year. We agreed to buy the bank's position for the full $150,000 they had invested, if they would make us the new loan.

---

14. *They can agree to discount the loan (short sale).* A short sale is similar to buying a loan at a discount, with two big differences. When you have a short sale, you are dealing with the owners of the property. You buy the property from them with a purchase contract with a purchase price less than the loan balance. The lender must then approve the contract. As we covered elsewhere, one key element of a short sale is that the seller cannot benefit from the sale. At the closing the lender will satisfy the loan. This may leave the original borrower still in the lender's debt.

There are times when you want the seller to be able to benefit from the sale. In that case, you want the lender to sell you the loan and assign it to you, not satisfy it.

15. *They can agree to sell you the loan.* There are circumstances where it is better to buy the existing loan than to pay it off. One case is if you want to keep the existing owners in the house. If they have improved their financial situation so that they can now begin making regular payments, you may want to buy the loan, not the house, and then renegotiate the loan with them. For example:

House value	$275,000
Balance on first mortgage	$190,000 – $10,000 in arrears
Your offer to the bank	$160,000 cash for the mortgage

You agree to renegotiate with the owners to allow them to start making payments of $1,500 for five years with a new interest rate of 10 percent, and the balance due in full in five years. At that time, they would owe you $225,000 with accrued interest. If there are other junior loans and liens, you don't want to just pay off a first mortgage, as that would put the old second mortgage in first position. Example:

House value	$275,000
Balance on first mortgage	$160,000
Balance on second mortgage	$60,000
Balance on lien	$30,000

If you pay off the first for $160,000, then the $60,000 second mortgage is now in first position and the $30,000 lien is in second position. The junior lenders will be hard to negotiate with if they are certain that they will be paid. As in the above example, you could renegotiate with the existing owners and then benefit from any discount that you can negotiate on the existing loans. The holders of the $60,000 second and $30,000 lien would probably be receptive to offers of 50 percent or even less. From the lender's standpoint the result is the same if it sells the loan or gets paid off. In both cases it receives cash and gets rid of a bad loan.

Banks sell loans all of the time. They are often sold in bulk through the mortgage banking department in the bank. You can buy a loan from a bank, but make sure that the bankers understand that you want an assignment of that loan, not a satisfaction of it. You will probably have to talk to a senior loan officer to make this deal.

16. *They can agree to lease you the property with an option to buy.* Although this would be a last choice for most lenders, it's better for them than owning and managing a property. Private lenders will be more receptive to this offer than bankers. However, bankers have leased property that they foreclosed on trying to generate some income. They have also sold with lease options, so it's not that they can't make this deal; they would rather get out of title. With that said, it may be a good negotiating strategy to make a lease option offer to a lender who you know wants badly to sell, then follow it up with a low-ball cash offer.

13

Nine Things That Make Lenders Nervous

When you are looking at a house that is headed for foreclosure, you need to look at it through the eyes of a lender. Often the lender is far away and relying on another to tell him about the condition and value of the house.

Remember that a picture is worth a thousand words, and nowadays with digital photography the picture is free. I looked at a house today that had been abandoned by the owners. The grass was several feet high, the water in the open pool too thick for me to see through to the bottom, and the fence surrounding the pool in pretty bad shape. I took some beautiful pictures. The old tires stacked in the porch almost looked like someone was about to start a fire.

While it is not ethical to PhotoShop a picture to make it look worse, the good news for potential buyers is that many foreclosures look pretty grim just the way they are. Not all foreclosures are scary, and the ones that look frightening can often be brought back by getting a crew in for a couple of days, hauling the junk away, and cleaning and painting.

When you find a house that will make a lender nervous, it's often a real opportunity. Lenders don't sell every foreclosure cheap. In fact, they get their money back on many of them that are in good shape. They often take the large losses on the ones that need work.

Here are situations that signal opportunity for you as a buyer of a foreclosure:

1. *An abandoned house, asking to be vandalized.* Empty houses are trouble waiting to happen. Look for empty houses in neighborhoods where you want to buy. Always investigate them. When you find one owned by a lender, research, and if you like the house, make an offer you really like.

2. *A house that has been damaged.* Houses that need a lot of work fall into two categories: trouble and more trouble. If a house has been abused, it can take a lot of work and time to put it back in good condition. What's involved are not simply cosmetic repairs like painting and installing carpeting. The repairs needed are like fixing broken door frames, broken windows, damaged cabinetry, and abused plumbing. This work requires skilled professionals: electricians, plumbers, and carpenters.

   Before you make an offer on a house that needs significant repairs, know how much you will have to invest before you can rent or sell the house. Guess high, and round higher. Cost and time overruns are the rule, not the exception, in rehabbing.

3. *A house that is not complete.* Lenders hire inspectors to confirm that houses that are being built have reached certain stages of completion. Sometimes a lender funds a loan and the builder runs out

of money and cannot complete the house. Then the lender will be stuck with a house that it cannot either sell or rent to a user. This is a situation that is an opportunity for a buyer who can assess the amount of work that needs to be completed.

I have bought houses in various stages of completion. If you ask, you can borrow the money to complete the house, plus get concessions on both the interest rate and payment schedule. Completing a new house is less risky than repairing a damaged house. If a house needs cabinets, floor covering, and painting, you can get firm bids from contractors to complete the work. The other good news is that when the housing market softens, often contractors are looking for work, so you can get this work done at a good price and quickly.

4. *Environmental issues: mold, lead paint, buried oil tanks, etc.* A lender does not want to own a property with environmental problems that might someday involve him in a lawsuit. To avoid a foreclosure where the lender could obtain title if no one bids, the lender will renegotiate the terms of the loan or sell the loan to you at a discount.

Some environmental problems cost a lot to remedy; some, very little. Some are more dangerous to people (lead paint) than others (a buried oil tank). Get good advice from a local contractor who solves these problems regularly, and then make an offer that pays you well for your extra effort. Local lenders have taken 70 percent discounts on loans that were secured by curable problems.

5. *A house occupied by scary-looking tenants (with big, scary-looking dogs).* Lenders are professionals, but like most people, they do not seek or relish confrontations with hostile people. A tenant in a property that has been foreclosed is rarely friendly. Some are not civil. Many have been living there for free for months.

When confronted or intimidated by a tenant, the lender will often make you a great deal. There is a civilized solution to a hostile tenant: You simply go through the eviction process and at some point the sheriff will move that person out. The risk you take is that the property may not be in pristine condition when the tenant leaves.

Often, if you approach the tenant with an offer of money, that person will leave. He knows that his days of free rent are numbered, and a new face offering him real cash to move out will often help him avoid an eviction. Start the eviction proceeding and have the tenant served with a notice before you approach him. Sometimes you can pay a little extra money and have the eviction notice delivered by a uniformed deputy. It lets the tenant know that you are serious. Now your offer of $500 to be out by this weekend with all of his stuff looks better. Don't pay him until he is completely out and has relinquished the keys. Then immediately change the locks.

6. *A house with a pool, especially a pool with water too thick to see through to the bottom.* A pool in poor condition is almost as much of a liability as an environmental problem. An owner of such a pool will have liability that, at the very least, will be very expensive to insure. Some lenders will completely cover a pool with lumber and wire mesh to keep someone from falling into it. This is an expensive undertaking, and the result looks really bad.

    Like other problems, pools are relatively easy to bring back to standard condition. All it takes is money and a pool company that knows its business. You can probably negotiate a discount from the lender that will be several times the actual cost of restoring the pool.

7. *A house that is not up to code.* Building codes change, and insurance companies pay attention. They may require the electrical or roofing system to be improved to comply with current building

codes before they will insure the house. Learn about the requirements in your local insurance market. Some companies will require a certificate from a house inspector or contractor that states the condition of the house.

When you find a lender stuck or about to be stuck with an uninsurable house, make an offer that pays you well for solving the problem. New wiring or a new roof does not increase the value of the property by as much as it costs. Deduct the cost of the improvement from your offer.

8. *A property that is nonconforming.* Nonconforming property is property that is not in compliance with current zoning or building codes. If the existing structure is destroyed or substantially damaged, the local government may require you to rebuild to comply with the current rules and regulations. A good example is a house that is built near the coast. The government changes the setback requirements, requiring houses to be set back a certain distance from the shore. If the house is destroyed, it will not be allowed to be rebuilt in its current location.

   Another example is an existing duplex built on a lot that is now zoned for just one living unit. If it is destroyed, you could not rebuild the duplex; you could only build a house.

   When a lender has a loan on a nonconforming property, point it out to her. It may inspire her to discount or renegotiate the loan.

9. *A house that is expensive to insure or maintain.* Some properties are at high risk from an insurance standpoint. They may be far from a fire hydrant or in an area with a high occurrence of fires. Or they may be in an area where vandalism is common. Other houses may be fragile and expensive to maintain. Lenders are not eager to invest more money in a foreclosed house. They have the

right to protect their investment and will occasionally board up windows and secure the house. However, they do not want to write a check to put a new roof on a property or replace windows. When you find a house that fits this profile, know that the lender is eager to make you a deal, and adjust your offer accordingly.

All of these factors make a lender more eager to do business. The lender may talk tough and say that he won't discount, but when you find a house that you want to own and it fits in one of these categories, make him an offer you like. Your best deals will be with a lender who has decided that day to get rid of this property.

14

Buying from Sellers in Bankruptcy

It would be appropriate if this chapter were numbered 7, 11, or 13. All three of these numbers are different chapter numbers of the Federal Bankruptcy Code, and they may be used by borrowers to interrupt the process of foreclosure.

The Bankruptcy Abuse Prevention and Consumer Protection Act of 2005 changed the law to prevent common abuses of the bankruptcy system. Before this statute, debtors could run up significant credit card debt and then file bankruptcy to discharge those debts. Some homeowners in financial trouble would file bankruptcy over and over again to stop a foreclosure. The new law requires some debtors to choose a plan to repay their debts over time (Chapter 13) rather than just liquidating their assets (Chapter 7). It also requires credit counseling, and perhaps most importantly, it makes their attorney responsible for the accuracy of their financial representations. This additional burden on attorneys has increased the cost of filing a bankruptcy and will discourage serial filings. In fact if a debtor files, the case is dismissed, and the debtor files again (a common trick), the debtor can lose the protection of the bankruptcy law, including the ability to stop a foreclosure.

Another change in the 2005 act is the limit on the amount of protection a creditor receives on his or her homestead. Some states like Florida and Texas give a homeowner unlimited homestead protection against creditors. A debtor in trouble could move to Florida, buy a big house, and file bankruptcy. Under the previous law, the creditors could not have access to the equity in the house. The new law requires a debtor to own the house for 1,215 days prior to filing for bankruptcy or be subject to a $125,000-per-owner exemption. That applies only to the equity in a property, not the value. In addition, now there is a 10-year "look back" if the debtor has liquidated other property and used the proceeds to buy a home in anticipation of bankruptcy.

It costs money to file a bankruptcy. The forms that you need are available online, but there are still fees to pay, and most people will not fill out and file their own forms. Many who consider hiring a lawyer to file bankruptcy find that they cannot afford the attorney's fees. As previously noted, this number will be increasing because of the new law and because fewer attorneys choose to take the risk associated with this field of practice.

Although bankruptcies increase when the economy stutters, bankruptcies affect only a small number of property owners who need to sell.

My knowledge of bankruptcy is, thankfully, limited. In 35 years of investing, only a few of the sellers I purchased from have filed bankruptcy. And in every case, we were able to complete the purchase. One person with whom I co-owned property filed bankruptcy unrelated to the property. I simply bought his interest for what he had paid for it. Although the amount I paid was less than the market value, my purchase provided some needed cash and the court approved the sale.

How to Deal with a Seller Who Files Bankruptcy

When a seller files bankruptcy, it is not necessarily a bad thing. Just the mention of bankruptcy will scare off a lot of competition, and that is a good thing. If you will learn a little about how the system works and then be ready when a property becomes available, then you can buy at a good price.

A homeowner or investor who files bankruptcy may be trying to buy a few weeks or months of time with which to sell and find another place to move. The person probably files bankruptcy to stop an imminent foreclosure. If she has a lot of equity, she can probably stall the foreclosure sale for many months. If she has little equity, then the lender may get the stay that bankruptcy imposes lifted and continue the foreclosure.

If you are buying a house with some equity, you can make the same type of offer that you would if there were no bankruptcy. It can include terms and even involve the exchange of another property for the person's house.

If the seller has little equity, you can make a short-sale offer or you can take another approach and offer to buy the loan directly.

Bankruptcy allows a debtor to renegotiate the payment of his debts or just throw in the towel, surrender all of his assets, and let his creditors liquidate them and divide what they own.

Different Creditors Have Different Interests

There are two types of creditors in a bankruptcy: secured and unsecured. Secured creditors are those who have a recorded interest against a property. They are treated differently (and better) than unsecured creditors. A secured creditor is typically a mortgage lender with a recorded loan document. An unsecured creditor has no recorded lien attaching a particular property. Often unsecured creditors include credit card companies, hospitals, and other merchants or service providers who have claims.

Generally, secured creditors will be paid from the sale of the asset they have as security, and unsecured creditors will receive a prorated amount from any other assets, including any equity left in the property after the loan is paid off. One purpose of bankruptcy is to give the debtors some time to market a property so that they or their creditors can receive more money from the sale.

Three Types of Bankruptcy and Their Advantages

There are three primary types of bankruptcy:

1. Chapter 7, Liquidation
2. Chapter 11, Reorganization
3. Chapter 13, Adjustment of debts

The following is a brief explanation of these three types of bankruptcy, which is extracted and edited from the U.S. Courts Web site. For much more information, visit the Web site: http://www.uscourts.gov/bankruptcycourts/bankruptcybasics/html.

Chapter 7, Liquidation

Liquidation is the sale of a debtor's nonexempt property and the distribution of the proceeds to creditors. Exempt property is certain property owned by an individual debtor that the Bankruptcy Code or applicable state law permits the debtor to keep from unsecured creditors. For example, in some states the debtor may be able to exempt all or a portion of the equity in the debtor's primary residence (homestead exemption), or some or all "tools of the trade" used by the debtor to make a living (for example, auto tools for an auto mechanic or dental tools for a dentist). The availability and amount of property the debtor may exempt depends on the state the debtor lives in. A Chapter 7 bankruptcy case does not involve the filing of a plan of repayment as in Chapter 13. Instead, the bankruptcy trustee gathers and sells the debtor's nonexempt assets and uses the proceeds of such assets to pay holders of claims (creditors) in accordance with the provisions of the Bankruptcy Code. Part of the debtor's property may be subject to liens and mortgages that pledge the property to other creditors.

Chapter 11, Reorganization

A Chapter 11 debtor usually proposes a plan of reorganization to keep its business alive and pay creditors over time. People in business or individuals can seek relief in Chapter 11. Often it involves a corporation or partnership.

An appointed bankruptcy trustee will closely supervise a reorganization plan. It is likely to involve a lot of an attorney's time and be costly to file and administer. Usually, only businesses or individuals with significant assets that are likely to survive use Chapter 11.

Chapter 13, Adjustment of Debts

A common form of individual bankruptcy is Chapter 13, which allows a debtor to renegotiate payments on his or her existing debt, much like a debt consolidation loan, except the trustee will collect from the debtor and pay the creditors. Individuals will have no direct contact with creditors while under Chapter 13 protection.

It is also called a "wage earner's plan"; it enables individuals with regular income to develop a plan to repay all or part of their debts. Under this chapter, Section 1322(d) of the Code, debtors propose a repayment plan to make installments to creditors over three to five years. If the debtor's current monthly income is less than the applicable state median, the plan will be for three years unless the court approves a longer period "for cause." If the debtor's current monthly income is greater than the applicable state median, the plan generally must be for five years. In no case may a plan provide for payments over a period longer than five years. During this time the law forbids creditors from starting or continuing collection efforts.

Chapter 13 offers individuals a number of advantages over liquidation under Chapter 7. Perhaps most significantly, Chapter 13 offers individuals an opportunity to save their homes from foreclosure. By filing under this chapter, individuals can stop foreclosure proceedings and may cure delinquent mortgage payments over time. Nevertheless, they must still make all mortgage payments that come due during the Chapter 13 plan on time. Another advantage of Chapter 13 is that it allows individuals to reschedule secured debts (other than a mortgage for their primary residence) and extend them over the life of the Chapter 13 plan. Doing this may lower the payments. Chapter 13 also has a special provision that protects third parties who are liable with the debtor on "consumer debts." This provision may protect co-signers. A homeowner in Chapter 13 is still able to refinance the house and pay off all of his debts, if a loan is available to him.

A Stay of Foreclosure

A stay of foreclosure, also called an "automatic stay," provides a period of time in which all judgments, foreclosures, collection activities, and repossessions of property are suspended and may not be pursued by the creditors on any debt or claim that arose before the filing of the bankruptcy petition. This stay goes into effect immediately upon the filing of a bankruptcy.

Lenders can request relief from the stay if they can convince the judge that the property is deteriorating and their security is in jeopardy, or if they can show that there is no equity above their loan.

Bidding Strategy

In a bankruptcy, often the trustee will handle the sale of property to raise cash to pay other creditors. The bankruptcy trustee will sometimes solicit an offer on property. A solicited offer is called a "stalking horse" bid. It is solicited in the hope that another party will make a higher offer. If you make this first offer, you can attach conditions, such as that the next offer must be at least 10 percent higher, or that you have the right to bid again if there is a higher bidder. Before you bid you might want to order an owners and encumbrances (O and E) report to see who the creditors are. The O and E report will show you the names and amounts of all existing liens. This may help you determine your offer. If the property has one large lien for 70 percent of the value, you may bid just above that lien amount.

Creditors can object to a sale if they feel it is not selling for enough. Your offer does not have to be all cash, but like buying a foreclosure from a lender, cash offers have the advantage. If you have no serious competition, make an offer with terms that you like.

When It Is Worth Pursuing a Property in a Bankruptcy

When you find a house or other property that you think is an opportunity, if you have researched the amount owed and feel that an offer will solve a problem for the debtor, you should make the offer. After a foreclosure sale is canceled because of the bankruptcy filing, the primary lender on the property and other lien holders have lower expectations. Although your offer will need to be approved by the bankruptcy court, the court often responds quickly, and if yours is the only offer, you have a good chance of buying a bargain.

A Deed from a Bankruptcy Trustee Is Clean Title

One advantage of buying from a bankruptcy trustee rather than at a foreclosure sale is that the trustee's deed you will receive will be free and clear of all liens against the debtor. You will be buying the property in as-is condition, because the trustee will not warrant the condition of the house.

Those who have claims against the property or the debtor can only look to the cash received from the sale, which will be divided among all those who make legitimate claims. Bankruptcy can be used to solve sticky title problems. When title is issued from a bankruptcy trustee, it is a clean title and can extinguish nearly every claim against the title. Check with your attorney, but an entity that owns a property with title problems may consider filing a bankruptcy and selling the property as a solution.

If you find yourself as a creditor in a bankruptcy, recognize that the courts move quickly when they have offers. As a creditor, you may have five days to respond or to object to an offer made on a property owned by the debtor. You may want to make a higher offer, and if you are a secured creditor, you can use your debt as part of your offer.

15

Borrowing to Buy Your First Foreclosure

Using Leverage Safely

Perhaps the greatest advantage you have when investing in real estate is the ability to borrow a large portion of the purchase price on terms that are self-liquidating. If the purchase is financed well, the income from the investment will pay off your debt.

Some buyers borrow more than the property will repay or borrow from lenders who charge high interest rates. If you buy a property that produces a 5 to 6 percent net return, then you need to be wise enough not to borrow more than you can repay with that income.

For example: You can buy a house worth $240,000 for $200,000 from a seller who has little time to wait for a higher offer. The house will rent for $1,500 a month, and the expenses of taxes, insurance, and maintenance are about $500 on an average month, so your net income available to repay debt is $1,000 a month. You can repay the following amounts at these interest rates with $1,000 a month.

Amount	Payment	Loan Terms
$200,000	$1,000	6% interest-only loan
$166,791	$1,000	30-year amortizing 6% interest rate loan
$150,307	$1,000	30-year amortizing 7% interest rate loan
$136,283	$1,000	30-year amortizing 8% interest rate loan

When you borrow at higher rates, the amount that you can borrow and repay with the same payments drops rapidly.

Buying real estate with leverage can be risky if you don't have a good understanding of how leverage works. If you do, then like Donald Trump, you can take on hundreds of millions of dollars of debt without risking your personal assets or losing sleep at night. Both personal assets and sleep are important.

There are two fears that prevent more people from making large profits in real estate. One is their fear of debt and another is fear of management. Knowledge is your best weapon against fear. Learn as much as you can about borrowing and managing, and they won't hinder your investing.

Be conservative when doing your projections. The house may not produce positive cash flow in the first year or two. That's okay, if you made a good deal and have the cash reserves to carry it. For example, if you buy a house worth $250,000 for $200,000, and the net rent that you collect (after your expenses) leaves you $250 a month short of your loan payment, you are investing another $250 a month, or $3,000 a year, into the house.

Borrowing to Buy Your First Foreclosure

Amount	Payment	Loan Terms
$200,000	$1,199	30-year amortizing 6% interest rate loan
$200,000	$1,331	30-year amortizing 7% interest rate loan

If the house appreciates at an average rate of 4 percent over the next few years, the appreciation will be $10,000 per year. When you sell, you will recover your $3,000 annual investment plus $7,000 a year in appreciation, plus the $50,000 profit you made when you bought the house. That is a great deal — as long as you can afford to make the additional investment.

Use a Hybrid Loan to Reduce Your Payments

By combining a bank loan, which has a relatively low affordable payment, with a loan that you will owe the seller and pay him back when you sell, you can reduce your payments to an amount that will be covered by the net rental income. Using the same house as an example:

Purchase price $200,000

New or existing bank loan : $150,000 payable $998 per month amortizing over 30 years at 7% interest rate

Loan to seller: $50,000 with no payments or interest, due upon the sale of the property or in 10 years.

16

Contract Negotiation

When you are buying a foreclosure, typically time is short. If the seller needs to sell and close in a day or two, you need to be able to prepare a contract that you and the seller can understand and agree to. Knowledge of contracts is important. When you make a written offer, you need to make an offer that gives you some protection yet is acceptable to the seller.

The Purchase Contract

There are no standard purchase contracts. Brokers, attorneys, title companies, and some buyers and sellers all create their own contracts. Although these documents may have similarities, it is a mistake to think that they are alike. Contracts are governed by state law, and although all states (except Louisiana) have real estate laws that have evolved from British common law, each state is unique.

The statute of frauds is widely applied to real estate contracts and requires that contracts for buying, selling, leasing, and financing real estate be in writing to be enforceable. You can have an oral contract, but it is not enforceable, so either party can refuse to close without penalty.

Key Points You Want to Cover in a Purchase Contract

There are many reasons to have a well-written contract other than having an agreement that you can enforce:

1. *You want all parties to understand, agree to, and remember the terms of your agreement*. People sometimes have short or faulty memories. To avoid renegotiating a deal, you need a written agreement that both parties understand and are bound by.

2. *You may need to show the contract to a lender*. Often you will reach an agreement with someone to buy her home and the agreement will call for you to take title subject to or assume their existing debt. The terms of this agreement will need to be shown to and perhaps explained to both the lender involved and the closing agent or attorney.

3. *Loans, even loans that require the lender to approve a new purchaser, can be assumed with the lender's permission*. When lenders already own more property than they want, they would rather let a new buyer continue to make the current payments than foreclose on a loan.

Contract Negotiation

In addition, your contract should state that the sellers give the buyers the right to contact and negotiate with the lenders. If you are buying a property with one or more loans in default, you only want to buy if you can make a deal with the lenders that allows you to make a profit. Your contract would then state that "the buyers have the right to contact any lender or lien holder with the intent of renegotiating the existing debt, and the closing on this property will be subject to the buyer renegotiating the debt to his satisfaction before the date of closing."

4. *The closing agent or closing attorney needs to be able to understand the agreement.* A closing is the event at which the sellers give you a deed and possession of the property and you give them any money due them. You will pay the costs of closing and sign documents, if needed, to acquire a new loan or to transfer the responsibility for the existing loan. The terms of your purchase as well as the specific terms of any debt that you will owe the sellers after closing need to be in the contract.

5. *As a buyer, you want to limit your requirement to perform on the contract.* If you change your mind for any reason and decide not to buy this property, you want to be able to walk away from the deal with only a small, if any, loss.

Most contracts prepared by a broker or attorney will give the seller the right to force the buyer to perform on a contract. The clause or paragraph may state that if the buyer does not perform, then he will lose his deposit and be responsible for attorney's fees and other monetary damages.

You want your "damages," called "liquidated damages," to be limited to your deposit, and you don't want to make a big deposit. In fact, several brokers in my town do not require any deposit on a purchase offer.

One argument for not making a large deposit is your ability to close quickly. Look for sellers who are in a hurry. They will make you the best deals. It's not unusual for me to close on a house purchase in only a week after I sign the contract. When you offer to close in a week or two, often only a small deposit will be required. If you want sellers to accept a contract with a long-term closing, which requires them to make more loan payments, then they will typically ask you for a bigger deposit.

6. *Sellers will agree in the contract to give you title (a deed) to the property at the time of closing.* The contract should state that the title is good and insurable, which means that a title insurance company will give you a policy that insures that the deed the sellers have given you has clear title.

7. *A contract should give you the right to inspect the house and grounds and give you access for that purpose.* Don't be shy about asking for access, and know that some sellers are not beyond hiding defects under a rug or behind a dresser or mirror. An empty house is the easiest to inspect; it is to your advantage to buy an empty house for many reasons. Having great access is just one of those reasons.

Have a professional inspector meet you at the house and follow her around noticing what she notices and digging in a little if you find anything that makes you nervous.

8. *Your contract should list what is included in your purchase.* Appliances, window treatments, fans, mirrors, and anything else like a lawnmower should be itemized on your contract. It should also state that the house will be empty (pay attention during your inspection for anything environmentally troubling) and all trash will be removed from the property prior to closing. If the sellers simply pile everything in the front yard, you may have to pay to have it removed.

Using a Broker's Contract

Brokers often have an office contract that they want to use. The contract is often biased toward the broker and the party the broker represents, typically the seller. This type of contract is reasonably fair and balanced, but be aware that the seller may have some advantages.

Brokers and attorneys print or type up elaborate contracts. They would prefer that you sign them just as they are. You need to read them carefully, however, and then change anything on that contract by simply marking through the words that you want to change, and writing in and initialing the change.

Another way to change a contract is to add an addendum. See the addendum in the appendix that gives a buyer more flexibility and protection when using a standard broker contract. Brokers will try to get you to use their contract when making an offer through their office.

The Purchase Contract When You Are Dealing Directly with the Sellers

Always ask sellers if they have a contract that they want to use. If they have one, it may be from an office supply store, or it may be a copy of a contract that they used before or that a friend gave them. Be especially careful if the contract is a copy of a previously used contract. The sellers may not understand it, but you should read it carefully to make sure you do. Don't be shy about making changes.

If they have a contract, let them use it, and ask them to explain it to you. It is a good idea to have sellers fill out the blanks in any contract in their own handwriting, adding any special clauses. If they write it down and it is their contract, they will understand the deal that they are making. You can then make a copy, and both the buyers and sellers can sign both copies.

When No One Has a Purchase Contract

When you find homeowners who are behind in their payments, often they have not thought through the process of selling their house and will not have a contract. You should have a purchase contract that you are comfortable with and that is simple and easy to understand. Many sellers have never actually read a contract (even when they bought), and they will be intimidated by a contract that has pages of fine print.

The purpose of the contract is not to have a bulletproof document that will stand up in court. As a practical matter, if sellers change their mind and the only way you can get them to close is to hire an attorney and take them to court, you are better off walking away from the deal and finding another, more willing seller. It could take you many months to resolve a contract dispute and require you to invest thousands of dollars in attorney's fees. Even if you are in the right, the outcome is not certain. *Although you would not tell sellers that you do not plan on enforcing a contract, you will buy more houses at better prices if you use a simple contract.* This contract might not put you in as strong a position in a court of law, if you had to go there, but your strategy should be not to go to court at all. I have never forced a seller to close.

Case Study: The Importance of Using a Simple Contract

The seller and buyer had agreed on a price and terms, so the buyer asked his attorney to draw up a contract for the purchase that reflected the agreed-on price and terms. When the contract was presented to the seller, it was many pages long and contained dozens of paragraphs of legal phraseology unintelligible to a nonlawyer. The seller refused to sign because he was certain that in some of the obtuse language were conditions that might be costly to him. The buyer was upset because he thought they had a deal, but the paperwork got in the way. The seller received another offer for less money presented on a simple, easy-to-understand contract, and he accepted it.

Lesson: Use the simplest contract appropriate for the situation. If the offer is easy to understand and the paperwork clear and understandable, you are far more likely to get an acceptance of your offer.

When You Are Buying Directly from a Bank

Occasionally you will find a bank-owned property not listed with a broker. Banks, especially out-of town banks, typically list properties on which they foreclose with local brokers.

When you buy directly from bankers, they may want to use the bank's contract, which is typically short and clear. Most bank contracts have the buyer purchasing the house in its as-is condition without warranting or disclosing anything. The bankers may agree to pay some closing costs, and everything is negotiable, but typically you will make such a good deal on price that you won't mind paying for some repairs and costs. You can get access to the property for inspections, and you should inspect carefully.

Inspection Clauses

Every contract you sign should give you the right to inspect the property. Even when you are buying from a bank and its contract requires you to take it in as-is condition, you still want to inspect. If the house needs a lot of work, you want to find out that fact *before* you close, not after.

A contract can require the sellers to make repairs that are found in an inspection or allow them to cancel the contract and refund the buyer's money. As a buyer, you want the right to walk away if you find anything that you don't like. If the inspection finds minor problems and you have made a good deal, don't lose your good deal because you ask for one more thing. If you find bigger problems, and you have the right to walk away, offer to buy at a lower price to compensate you for the repairs that must be made.

Inspections

After you have an agreement to buy subject to inspection, have the utilities turned on and have a professional inspector meet you at the property and test everything. Sellers who have lost their home to a lender may be mad enough to sabotage a house. Test every faucet, every drain, every electrical switch and plug, and, of course, any appliances, furnaces, and air-conditioning units.

Case Study: What We've Found at Inspections

I have bought houses that had holes shot through the roof! The holes were small enough that they could have been easy to miss. Other sellers have chopped holes in drywall and taken all of the plumbing fixtures, including the toilets. After buying one house at a foreclosure sale, I immediately drove to the house and found the neighbors digging up the bushes and small trees in the yard of the house I had just purchased. When I asked them what they were doing, they said that the owners had just left and, besides giving away everything in the house, they gave the neighbors the landscaping.

An inspection won't protect you against the irrational acts of a fore-closed owner, but if the house is available to inspect, you can find out what work the house needs, and even introduce yourself to the neighbors. It may save you some landscaping.

Loans and Loan Documents

Most house buyers borrow the money to buy the house from a bank or other conventional lender. Some buyers arrange owner financing with the sellers. Others may obtain a loan from the Federal Housing Administration (FHA) or the U.S. Departments of Veterans Affairs (a "VA loan"). All of these loans are secured by a mortgage or deed of trust, which gives the lender first (if it's a first mortgage or Trust Deed)claim against the property. The claim that these instruments have against the house depends on the order of their recording. The first instrument that is recorded becomes a first lien or mortgage or trust deed.

The mortgages or deed of trusts used by institutions or FHA or VA are not all the same, but they all have been prepared by attorneys with the thought of providing the maximum protection to the lender.

Mortgages or deeds of trust prepared by sellers may have fewer words and fewer protections for the lender, but they are often based on the commercial forms that the banks use.

When buying a house in foreclosure, an advantage is that the current lender has a problem just as the seller does. The seller can't afford the house payments, but the lender does not want to own the house.

Recognizing this quandary allows you to negotiate with a lender who has an existing loan that is in default. Be aware that you do not have to pay this loan off or get a new loan to buy a property when the lender does not want the property.

Any time that you are buying a property that has an existing loan in place, you want to read the loan documents to see to what the borrower-owner has agreed. You will be bound by the terms of the existing loan if you take title to the house and simply begin making payments. You may want to renegotiate the terms of the existing loan, and the best time to do this is before you close.

Closing Statements

A closing statement is the document that shows you the money in the transaction. In the hundreds of closings I have participated in, only a handful have had closing statements without errors. Some were worth many thousands of dollars to me. Because nearly every closing statement is wrong, insist on getting a copy of it before the closing, and review it carefully. I ask the closing agent to fax or e-mail it to me the day before the closing.

When you make offers to a seller who is in financial distress, it is wiser to do so in a way that guarantees the seller a certain amount of "walk-away" money. This would be a "net" offer and would override the traditional prorations of taxes and insurance and would have the buyer paying all of the closing costs.

You should not make a net offer unless you have a comfortable margin built into your offer and you know the amount of the expenses that you are agreeing to pay. Also as a net offer does not ask the seller to make any repairs, you need to have a thorough inspection done and know the cost of any needed repairs.

To make a net offer you simply state in your purchase contract that "at the closing the seller will receive a check in the amount of $21,000 [fill in the real amount], and the buyer will pay all closing costs, acquire the real and personal property listed along with any existing impound accounts, and take the property in its 'as-is' condition and that there will be no prorations."

Impound accounts, often called "escrow accounts," are the amount over and above the interest and principle payment due each month that the lender collects. If you are buying a property and taking over a loan with an escrow amount balance, it is important to discuss it. The above language states that the account balance is included in the sales price. If that is your agreement, get the seller to sign a document that transfers that account to you and authorizes you to endorse any check issued by the lender.

Getting a Bill of Sale for Any Personal Property

While a deed transfers the ownership of the real estate, it does not transfer the ownership of any personal property that you are buying. Personal property that is included with a house purchase typically consists of appliances such as the refrigerator or washer and dryer, but anything that is easily removable from the house like drapes or other window treatments, mirrors, or light fixtures should be listed in the contract and then transferred by a bill of sale. Your accountant may advise you that you can write off or depreciate these items over a very short period, which may save you many dollars in taxes.

Items that are attached to the house are called "fixtures." Even though these are legally part of the property and transferred with a deed, it is better to list on the contract any fixture (like an expensive mirror or light fixture) that you want to buy as part of your purchase.

Only the seller is required to sign the bill of sale. The buyer should get the original and any warranties still in effect and any instruction manuals.

Getting All of the Keys during the Walk-Through

During closings, make sure you ask for all of the keys. It's best to have the sellers or brokers meet you at the house immediately prior to the closing and have them produce keys to all the locks and label them for you. They can hold on to them until the closing, but you want to get a key to every lock; you'll also want to walk through the house to make sure that the sellers have moved out all of their property and are ready to give you possession. In the event that they still have stuff in the house, either refuse to close until they are able to give you possession or agree to rent the house back to them and you'll hold back a significant security deposit. Know that some states, Georgia is one, require the owners to give up possession the day of closing and prohibit any type of lease back to the seller. In Georgia and other states with similar laws, do not close until you can get possession.

17

Beware the Con Artists: Eight Costly Foreclosure Scams

Distress attracts some interesting characters; not all of them are honest. Unfortunate homeowners can fall prey to scams. You would think that the vultures could find a victim with more to lose than someone behind on his or her payments.

Another group of cons preys on those who are trying to make a profit buying foreclosures. Rather than appeal to the fear of loss, these cons appeal to the greed of the buyers. Greed has a wide appeal. Imagine sending money to someone you have never met, just on the chance that you may collect a large amount of money. This is a common Internet scam, but it works with foreclosures too. Here are more scams that are in use; beware of them.

1. *Rent skimming*. Sometimes desperate homeowners will let a buyer take over their payments and deed the buyer their home without receiving a significant down payment. While this alone is not a

problem, the problem arises when the buyer, who has little or nothing invested, never makes a payment on the loan.

Now the sellers are in the worst possible position. They have lost possession and title to the house, so they can't live there or rent it, and they are still responsible for the loan. If the house goes into foreclosure, their credit will be affected.

Often, the skimmer will give the sellers a note secured by the house and promise to pay them when the house sells. Of course, he never intends to pay the note, and it also gets wiped out by the foreclosure.

Sometimes the rent skimmer will live in the house for free as long as he can. Other times he will rent the house, pocketing the rent without making the payments.

2. *Equity skimming.* A clever crook targets sellers with large equities and makes them what appears to be a good offer. This con artist agrees to pay 50 percent down if the sellers will agree to hold a note for the other 50 percent, payable on a schedule they negotiate. Now the clever part: The skimmer arranges a new first mortgage or trust deed for 80 percent of the property value, paying the sellers their 50 percent and putting the other 30 percent in her pocket. Now the skimmer has a house encumbered with a 130 percent loan. She rents the house and pockets the rents without ever making a payment on the loan. When the first forecloses, she typically just walks away with the cash, leaving the poor (*really* poor now) homeowners stuck with the prospect of having to write a big check to protect their second-mortgage position.

This is white-collar crime at its nastiest. This scenario is obviously fraud, but some states have passed specific laws that state that equity skimming is illegal. The State of Washington specifies that if you commit three acts of equity skimming in a three-year period, you are guilty of a felony, punishable with a fine up to $2,000 per transaction. That's like getting a $2 speeding ticket.

That's not much of a deterrent to keep some crook from defrauding a homeowner out of tens of thousands of dollars of equity. Unfortunately, if you sell your house to a skimmer, you probably won't get much help from your local authorities until it is way too late.

Equity skimming laws often apply only to owner-occupied homes. Investors are not protected. Be on your guard when selling investment property. Don't subordinate to a new loan without fully understanding the deal. Subordinating isn't always a bad idea, but it often is.

If you are anxious to sell a house, either your residence or an investment, recognize that you are so. Then be careful about becoming so eager to make a deal that you sell to a con man or woman. It's a gender equal opportunity.

3. *Selling a house that they don't own.* Some cons are incredibly bold. They offer to rent a house from a homeowner having trouble making his payments. They target an owner who is out of town or at least not in the immediate area. Shortly after renting it, they plant a For Sale sign in the front yard, advertising that it is for sale. They tell everyone who calls that they are behind on their payments and must sell this weekend. They will take the first $5,000 over their loan balance, which they tell them is only about half the value of the house. They then agree to take a deposit from all sellers who think that they have found the bargain of a lifetime. Of course, it's the weekend, so they can't close until Monday, but during that weekend, they collect as many deposits (cash; no checks please) as they can, and then they leave town with the money.

We have all heard that something that seems to be too good to be true usually is. Although occasionally you can actually buy a terrific bargain, never give a seller more cash than you are willing to happily lose. My limit is $100. If a seller won't take a check (until tomorrow when the banks open), it is better to pass than to give away thousands of dollars.

4. *Charging a homeowner a fee for no results.* Although there are good-hearted people trying to help homeowners in distress save their home, there are also opportunists preying on these same homeowners. Charging homeowners an up-front fee for the promise of interceding on their behalf with their creditors may not be illegal, but unless you are successful and save their house and credit, it is certainly not helpful to the already strug-gling homeowner.

If you are a pro and can produce results, then those results are worth something to a homeowner. An attorney may charge several hundred dollars an hour and spend four or five hours to resolve this type of issue. Hopefully, he or she would charge his or her lowest rate, given the circumstances, so the total bill might be around $1,000. Unfortunately, some who are not as skilled are charging five times that much to homeowners and are not producing results.

5. *Selling out-of-town foreclosures at inflated prices with promises of great profit.* If you live in a place that has a high-priced real estate market, you may have seen or even been approached by someone selling far cheaper houses in another part of the county. These houses are often foreclosures; the pitch is that you can buy for a bar-gain price and these properties will be professionally managed for you and you will immediately start earning cash flow profits.

Many "investors" buy these houses without ever looking at them. Unfortunately, this is often a scam where houses are sold at retail or even higher prices, with the promoter taking a large commission or profit up front. Buyers of these houses may be dismayed to learn that the rental market is not what has been represented.

Although real estate prices do vary widely throughout our country and around the world, common sense should kick in and tell you that free markets are somewhat balanced everywhere. A property may look cheap from afar because you don't know that market. Houses that are in stronger markets tend to appreciate more. If you live in an area with a strong market, learn to buy where you live. Many others have done so, and they have made a lot of money in your market. Resist the sales pitch to buy a property over which you have little or no control. Buying a property in a distant town nearly always results in a loss for the investor.

If buyers borrow to buy an out-of-state property, they need to know that in many states lenders will pursue borrowers if they default on a loan. Just walking away from a bad investment may not be an option. Likewise, you will have personal liability as the owner for claims of tenants, workers, and others. Insurance may or may not cover these claims.

6. *Selling out-of-town notes on property that are worth far less than the amount of the notes.* Often when markets slow down, sellers use owner financing to unload property to sellers who cannot qualify for bank financing. If the houses that are sold are well built and maintained and in a good neighborhood, hopefully the buyers will be able to qualify for a conventional loan and pay off the notes.

Some houses are not in good-enough condition or in good-enough neighborhoods to qualify for a bank loan. The only choice when selling these properties is to sell with owner financing, as the banks will not make a loan. Typically, these homes are older ones in disrepair.

Often when these houses are sold, they are sold to lower-income buyers at inflated prices. Typically, a house that is bought at a foreclosure sale for $10,000 may be sold for $49,900 with a very small down payment. These notes are then sold, to unknowing buyers at small discounts that give the buyers an attractive return. A $49,000 note may be offered for $40,000. A buyer may think that he has a bargain, when in fact he has purchased a $40,000 note secured by a house worth far less than that amount.

Never buy a note unless you have inspected the property and confirmed that it is worth more than the amount you are paying for the note. Don't just look at the paperwork created when the property was sold. It can be deceiving.

7. *Using a fraudulent appraisal or contract to get a loan.* When credit is loose and lenders are aggressively making loans, the lenders often either overlook or get fooled by a high appraisal. In a hot market, property is bought and sold for twice the original price, sometimes within weeks of the first sale. The appraiser defends the second higher sales price with inflated comparable sales, and the lender makes a loan based on the second sales price. For example, a buyer pays $2.5 million for a property. He sells it to a business associate the next week for $5 million without doing any work to the property. The new buyer borrows $4 million from a bank at the second closing. The seller then walks away (far away) with the $1.5 million loan proceeds, and the bank gets stuck with the property.

Whenever you are buying or lending against a property, research the sales history of the property. If you spot something suspicious—several sales in a short period of time, or large jumps in sales prices—be cautious. Maybe the property has been improved, or maybe the buyer bought at a deeply discounted price from a relative or distressed owner. Understand why the price has jumped before you write a check.

Beware the Con Artists: Eight Costly Foreclosure Scams

8. *Gang bidding at foreclosure sales.* My good friend, Bob Bruss, used to write about the "40 thieves" that populated the foreclosure sales in his area. Experienced buyers often attend foreclosure sales. Although they are not officially organized, they probably know each other. They can use this familiarity to take advantage of an outsider bidding on a property. A comparable situation would be playing poker with six other players who know each other well and play every week. When you sit in on their game, do you think your chances of winning are diminished?

A foreclosure auction is supposed to be unrestricted, and in fact it would be against the law to collude or conspire to rig the price. It would also be hard to prove that several bidders are working together to get the best prices for each of them. For example, if there were 10 properties being auctioned and there were five bidders, rather than bidding against each other and running up the price, they could decide to take turns bidding on the properties. With only one bidder per property, it will sell at a much lower price. If you show up and start to bid, they may bid against you just to run up the price on the property that you want.

Always establish a maximum price that you are willing to bid before the bidding starts at an auction. Don't pay attention to any side talk, as other bidders may be trying to scare you away or discourage you from bidding. Again, "chilling," or discouraging others from bidding a fair amount, is illegal, but it is hard to prove or enforce.

18

Getting a Good Title and Understanding Title Insurance

What, exactly, is a "good" title? When you buy real estate, you get a deed to the property from the previous owner, or if you buy a foreclosure in a judicial foreclosure state, you get a certificate of title from a judge. If you buy from a trustee, you will receive a trustee's deed. All of these can convey good title, but only a deed from a previous owner is likely to give you any recourse against that owner if there are claims against the title. If you get title from a judge or trustee, the burden is on you to research to see if everyone who had a claim against the title has been paid or his or her rights have been extinguished by a properly conducted foreclosure action.

Good Deeds, and Not-So-Good Deeds

When you are buying, you want a deed from an owner that contains warrantees or guarantees that the owner is conveying good title to you and that he will defend that title if others make claims against it. These deeds are called "warranty deeds" or "grant deeds" and have this particular language. As many deeds are now generated on a word processor, they may not be titled as "warranty or grant deeds," so you or your attorney need to make sure that this language is contained in the document.

A deed without any guarantees or representation of ownership from the owners is called a "quitclaim deed." These deeds are often used to clear title claims or to transfer property interest among family members or from an owner to a corporation or partnership. Because a quitclaim deed may or may not convey good title, and because the buyer has no recourse against the seller if he gets bad title, you should not accept one when you are buying.

Trustees and officers of the court who may execute documents that transfer title are not guaranteeing good title, so their deeds, like quitclaim deeds, make no representations or guarantees about the condition of the title. It's up to the buyer to know what he is buying.

Obviously, you will want an attorney on your team if you are buying a foreclosure or buying from anyone who will not stand behind the title.

Recording Deeds and Taking Possession of the Property

To protect yourself against fraud and future claims against the seller, you always want to immediately record your deed in the county where the property is located to give notice to the public that you are now the owner. An attorney or title company handling a closing should do this for you. If you don't record the deed, the title will still be held in the seller's name. If the seller is sued or someone records a lien or judgment against her, these liens could attach the property. A dishonest seller could actually sell the house to another person and also give him a deed. At that time, the first deed recorded will have a superior claim against the title.

In addition, you want to take actual possession, which means getting the keys and maybe changing the locks, or visiting the tenants and telling them that you are the new owner. This action protects you against a dishonest seller who may collect advanced rent or even sell to another.

Title Reports, Commitments, and Title Policies

Before you make an offer, you should get a report about the condition of the title; this is good detective work. A title report, often called an "owners and encumbrance (O&E) report," will state who the present-day owners are and to whom they owe money. These reports are inexpensive, typically in the range of $75 to $100. You can go one step further and order a blank title commitment. It would read to a "buyer to be named" and at a "price to be determined."

This report will give the proper legal description, name the current owners, and list the claims against the title that need to be cleared such as existing loan, liens, unpaid property taxes, and judgments against the current owners. In addition, the commitment may list easements of records such as utility easements. These can be important, as they may restrict your ability to build an addition or add a pool if they run through the middle of a lot. Other private easements may not show up on the records.

If there is a question about where the lot line is or perhaps the position of a driveway or fence, have the property surveyed. A survey should show both the property boundaries and any encroachments by the neighbors on your property.

At the closing, and before you pay the sellers and get a deed from them, you will get a title commitment from a real estate attorney or title company. This commitment is not an insurance policy, it is a commitment to insure, but it has a lot of value to you as the buyer. Title insurance policies, like most insurance policies, are often not read until you have a problem. Fortunately, title problems are relatively rare, and they are solvable. It just takes time and money.

The practical reason you buy title insurance is because your lender makes you do so. No one will make a loan unless you can prove you own the property and have clear title. Although title insurance is not a guarantee that you have clear title, it is an insurance policy that states that the underwriter will pay to clear the title if a claim is made.

When you buy and borrow, two title insurance policies are issued: one to the owner and one to the lender. The lender's policy is assignable if he sells the loan, which lenders frequently do. The owner's policy is not assignable, and if you transfer the house to another party, even to a family member or your own company, you may void your title insurance. Always check with your title insurance agent before you transfer title.

Bad Title Can Signal Opportunity

Sometimes a property will be taken off the market or a sale will fail to close because of a title problem. If you can recognize that that title problem can be easily solved, then you may be able to buy the property at a bargain price and then solve the problem.

Some title problems, like an improper spelling of a name, a failure of a spouse to join in signing a deed, or a judgment that was paid but not released, are easy to solve, if all parties will cooperate. Most people will sign a document clearing the title if they are asked nicely. If being nice doesn't work, the offering of a little money, like $250, often will.

Even these little problems may delay a closing, and in times of rising interest rates, might even cause a long-enough delay that a loan commitment could expire. When a buyer walks away from a deal, then often the seller will make you (the new buyer) a great deal.

Other title problems, like an estate improperly settled or a forgery on a previous deed or satisfaction, can take much longer to resolve. For example, if a house was owned by a husband and wife and the husband has had another person sign his wife's name at the closing, the real wife will want to get paid when she finds out that she has been defrauded. If there is title insurance, the title insurer has the responsibility to pay her and resolve the claim. However, they may not be able to agree to an amount, which would result in a lawsuit to determine how much she should be paid. This process could take months, if not years, to settle.

More complicated title issues involve estates that were not properly settled, so no one has the authority to sign a deed. Sometimes the heirs will simply continue living in the family house without spending the money necessary to probate the estate. When it is eventually sold, no one has the authority to sign the deed. Recently I acquired a house that was owned by a 12-year-old. She was the sole heir of her father when he died. A minor child cannot transfer title, so a guardian had to be appointed by the court who could sign for her. This process took nearly a year.

Properties with title problems can be purchased. A house in foreclosure can be bought subject to the loan, which is a big claim against the title. If the loan is in default, sometimes it will take months or longer to resolve. An Ohio homeowner recently stalled a foreclosure for 11 years by outwitting his lender and using the court system to his advantage. A lender may be willing to just sell the mortgage at a discount rather than pursue a foreclosure.

Case Study: House in Foreclosure and the Lender Is Not Responding

A homeowner was in default on two loans. He tried for a month to work out an agreement with his lender. He agreed to sell the house to me, subject to the existing loans. I took title and began negotiating with the lender. In the meantime, I rented the house to a tenant who wanted to buy the house. I made full disclosure to the tenant-buyer that the house was in foreclosure and that he might have to move on short notice. More than a year later I was able to work out a solution with the lender. During that time I could not deliver good title, but the tenant was content to rent, and he eventually bought the house from me.

Title Insurance Case Study: Buyer Uninsured

Jones bought a house from a seller for $1,000 down and took over his first mortgage loan with a $200,000 balance. The lender had title insurance on its loan, so Jones took a risk and did not purchase title insurance at the closing. After the closing, the seller's ex-wife claimed that she had an interest in the property. Jones had to negotiate with her and write her a check for her interest. His alternative was to walk away from his investment in the property. Although he had only paid $1,000, he thought his equity in the house was worth about $25,000, so he wrote the ex a check to buy her interest. The lender's policy would protect the lender, but not the buyer. Had Jones purchased an owner's policy, then the lender would have paid the claim.

Tenants Don't Do Title Searches

You can rent a house with less than perfect title. If the title condition may threaten the right of a tenant to occupy the house, make full disclosure when you rent the house.

Some title issues take years to resolve, and most buyers will not get involved because they do not understand the system and the risks and rewards involved. If you find a property with a serious title problem, sometimes you can buy it for next to nothing, and make a nice profit for solving the problem.

Solving Unsolvable Title Problems

A title problem that seems unsolvable or that is too expensive to solve in another way can be solved by filing a quiet title lawsuit. Some laws have specific statutes that govern quiet title. It is important to use real estate lawyers with experience in this area and to get good advice before pursuing this solution.

A quiet title suit, or suit to remove a cloud, typically must be filed by the owner. You would have to buy the property with the title problems before you could use this remedy.

A "cloud" is a claim against the title like an unsatisfied lien.

Properties bought at tax sales will not have insurable title, so a suit to quiet title is commonly used to clear off old claims of previous owners and lien holders.

Don't go looking for title problems. When one pops up, rather than just walking away from the property, look for a feasible solution. Most title problems can be solved with a little time and paperwork. A good real estate attorney or experienced title agent is an invaluable asset in solving these types of problems. They have seen them all.

19

Foreclosure Buying Checklist

The following are some things you need to do before buying a foreclosure. Keep this list handy, and go through the items, one by one, before you invest in any foreclosed real estate.

1. Identify the neighborhood where you want to buy.
2. Learn the laws in your state that apply to buying properties in foreclosure.
3. Get ready to buy: Identify your source of cash for down payment and closing costs, set up a line of credit, and contact investors who may fund your purchase.
4. Contact the neighbors who own property and begin looking for opportunity.
5. Form your plan of what you will do with the property if you buy it.

6. Once you find an opportunity, research values, rents, and the owners' situation.

7. Make an offer.

8. Contact the lenders, lien holders, and tenants. Negotiate!

9. Work closely with the closing agent to ensure that the lien holders have signed estoppel letters and are ready to close. (An estoppel letter is a document on which a buyer can rely that is signed by a lender or tenant, confirming either the current loan balance and terms, or lease amount and terms.)

10. Close and take possession (as allowed by your state laws). If tenants are in residence, introduce yourself and give them a letter with your name and address for paying the rent.

11. Buy insurance.

12. Get the title policy.

13. Check to see that the deed was recorded. The original deed should be returned to you, the buyer.

14. If a loan was renegotiated or modified, get a copy of the agreement and record it, if possible.

15. Rent or sell the house.

16. Only then look for your next deal. Build your wealth one house at a time.

20

How to Make the Decision to Rent or Sell

Before you make an offer on a house, you should ask the question, "If I get it, what will I do with it?" Sometimes a good deal happens pretty fast, and you buy a house just because it's a good deal. You may even plan to sell it but find a great tenant instead. Or you may try to rent it and have a buyer make you an offer that you can't refuse.

There are some houses that make good prospects for long-term rentals and others that you should definitely sell as quickly as possible. Here are some questions to ask yourself that will help you make the decision.

How Large Was the Down Payment You Made?

If you have a lot of cash invested in a house, then you may want to sell it to get back your cash. Your return on your investment will be lower with a large investment. The best houses to hold onto for long-term investments are the houses that you can buy with the least amount of your money invested. For example, if you buy a $200,000 house with a $10,000 down payment and it appreciates at an average rate of 5 percent a year, your average appreciation will give you 100 percent return on your investment. If you bought the same house with $50,000 down, the return due to appreciation drops to 20 percent. Of course, the terms of the financing of the house are just as important as the amount that you put down.

What Are the Terms of the Financing?

Sometimes the terms of the financing when you purchase a house are so good that you want to keep the house just to keep the financing. Low-cost financing allows you to either rent the property at a profit or sell to another party and carry "wraparound" financing. Wraparound financing allows you to leave the existing financing on the property while selling to a new buyer with financing with different terms.

I have purchased houses with owner financing that had interest rates ranging from 10 percent to as low as 0 percent. The lower-interest-rate loans often have shorter terms so that the loans pay off quickly. If your plan is to own several houses free and clear, then short-term, low-interest-rate owner financing can help you reach that goal more quickly.

Even bank loans with interest rates of 7 percent or lower can add value to a property. When you are buying a bank-owned property (or a property on which a bank has a loan in default but does not want to own), you have an opportunity to ask for low-cost financing. Sometimes the loan you are able to negotiate is so valuable that it is the reason that you buy the property.

Chart Showing How Loans Add Value to a Property

House Value $220,000, Monthly Rent $1,500, Net Rent* $1,000

Monthly Loan Amount	Interest Rate	Payments	Term	Value Added
$200,000	0%	$1,000	200 months	Yes
$200,000	6% Interest Only	$1,000	100 months	Yes
$200,000	5%	$1,061	40 years	Yes
$200,000	7%	$1,464	30 years	No

* After taxes, insurance, and maintenance

When you can negotiate financing with terms of 10 years or longer with payments that allow you to have immediate cash flow, then the financing adds value to the property. If the payments are higher than the cash flow that the property currently produces or when the term of the loan is shorter, you may have to sell or refinance before the property doubles in value. These terms do not add value.

Substituting Collateral

You can sometimes take a good loan with you to another property. It is called "substituting one collateral for another." If you buy a house from a seller who finances the purchase for you on good terms and then develop a good relationship because you always pay on time, then you may be able to move that loan to another property that you buy.

Suppose that you buy a house today for $150,000 with a $140,000 6 percent, 30-year loan. Five years from now you get a cash offer of $240,000 for the house, but you don't want to pay off the low-interest-rate loan. You could ask the lender if they would take a discount if you paid their loan off early and increase your profits.

Another option that is better for the seller is to move her loan to another house that you already own. Suppose you own another house worth about $240,000, with an $80,000 loan balance. You could ask your lender to move her loan to that house, and agree to pay off the existing first of $80,000 (using part of the $240,000 cash from your other offer). This would give the lender security, and because you are still making the payments, she would be comfortable. After you use $80,000 to pay off the smaller loan first, you would have about $160,000 before taxes to spend or to use to buy other property.

I have borrowed from many sellers, and some I have owed over the years were sad when I paid them off. They liked me owing them money because I always paid on time. They preferred the interest I paid them to the lower rate the bank pays, and they liked getting checks every month.

Can You Borrow Back Your Down Payment and Still Afford to Hold the House?

Sometimes you buy with a large down payment. The extreme example is when you buy for all cash. If you make a great deal because you pay all cash but can then borrow against the property on great terms, you may be able to borrow back all of the cash that you invested. When interest rates are low, this can allow you to both have a small investment in the property and have cash flow.

Although borrowing from banks when you buy a house is difficult, as they move too slowly (really good deals often close in a day or two), borrowing after you buy a house can be a good strategy if you plan on holding the house until it doubles in value. There is a significant cost of borrowing from a bank, typically 3 percent or more of the amount that you borrow, so if you plan on selling quickly you would not want to borrow and incur that cost.

Is the House a Good Candidate for a Rental?

Is the house on a quiet street surrounded by good neighbors? If so, it may attract excellent long-term tenants. Is the house well built and in good shape? You never want to rent a "high-maintenance" house. Some houses require a lot of attention because of their design, others because of low-quality materials used to build them. When you buy a house that is somewhat fragile, you want to sell it or trade it for a better long-term investment.

Is the House in Good Shape Now, or Will You Have to Invest More Cash and Fix It Up Before You Rent It?

Putting more cash into repairs is like making a bigger down payment. It increases your investment, drops your rate of return, and makes it a less attractive investment. Although you can sell on terms a house that needs work, it is harder to rent a house that needs work to a good tenant.

Will It Require a Lot of Maintenance?

You don't want to rent a house to a tenant at a fixed rate and then have to make a lot of expensive repairs. If the house needs work, have it done before you rent it. You will attract a better tenant and be able to collect more rent. If the amount needed to make the repairs is significant, sell it instead. Many buyers are willing to take on a project if you will finance the purchase for them.

Will It Probably Appreciate at a Better-Than-Average Rate?

This may be the most important question when deciding whether to rent or sell. You want to own houses in the areas of your town that have the best chance of appreciation. If the average appreciation rate in your town is 4 percent, probably some houses are going down in value, some are appreciating at the 4 percent rate, and others are appreciating at more than 4 percent. You want more!

Have You Learned How to Manage?

Although you can hire a manager, if you know what a good manager should produce, you will be able to manage your manager better. Managing your own properties has advantages and drawbacks.

Many people think that if you manage you need to be available to your tenants 24/7. There is a difference between managing a house and a motel. With a motel or even an apartment building, tenants are more demanding and look for a short response time when something breaks.

House tenants are more self-sufficient. You can give a house tenant a list of approved repair people and have them call them directly when they have a problem. This keeps you from getting the call at night or on a weekend and lets the tenant take responsibility for caring for the house. I never take repair calls after hours or on weekends.

An advantage of managing your own properties is that you can select the tenants that you want and look for those with long-term potential. Tenants who stay for several years are far easier to manage. Like a long-term employee, a long-term tenant learns the system and requires little supervision. Plus, when a tenant stays five years, you have five years of no vacancy and fewer repairs. Your repair bills will be higher in years when people move.

Can You Partner with a Good Manager?

My good friend Peter Fortunato (who teaches excellent classes on investing) dislikes managing but loves buying property. Whenever Pete buys a house, he finds an owner/manager in the areas where he is buying and makes a deal with that manager to share the profits when he sells the house. In return for half the profits the house makes, the manager has to take responsibility for all of the management. Pete does not want any other interaction with this house until it sells.

Pete looks for an experienced manager who owns several properties, so taking on one more is not a big deal for him. This manager will not be paid a commission but instead a share of the profits when the house is sold. This share could be significant, as much as half.

The manager benefits from Pete's purchase at a below-market price. Here are some numbers from a typical manager-owner share-the-profits deal:

House value:	$250,000
Pete's purchase price	$185,000
Terms of purchase	$10,000 down; $875 per month for 120 months (no interest)

Deal with manager: Lease the house from Pete for $875 and pay all other expenses (taxes, insurance, and maintenance) for 120 months at which time the house will be sold and they will split profits over the $185,000 purchase price 50/50. Although the manager may have to invest a little cash the first year, after that the house should make him money every year during the holding period.

Would You Rather Be Pete or the Manager in This Deal?

Pete has made a passive investment of $10,000 which will give him no cash flow for 10 years (120 months) but then pay him both the principal pay-down on the loan, $87,500, plus half the appreciation of the house. If there is no appreciation, he will make an $87,500 profit on his $10,000 investment. That's more than 20 percent-a-year compounded return.

The manager should make a little profit every year as he increases rents. If rents double in 10 years, he could be making several hundred dollars a month net profit by the end of the term. Plus he is entitled to half the profit between the ultimate sales price and the original purchase price of $185,000. If the house only appreciates another $85,000 in 10 years, that would result in a total profit of $140,000 ($325,000–$185,000), of which the manager would receive half. That is $70,000 for 10 years' work. If the work is renting one house, that's good pay.

Some would look at Pete's deal and cringe at the amount of profit Pete is giving away just to get a manager. Another less expensive alternative would be to rent the house cheap until the market turns around. If you advertise a house that would normally rent for $900 a month for $795 a month, you should have no trouble finding a tenant. If you are selective and pick a tenant who will take good care of the property, you have hired a manager for about $100 a month. That's a cheaper solution that requires you to invest some time, but not much.

Buy Fast, Sell Slow

Two of my more successful students operate a profitable real estate investment firm in California. They specialize in buying houses quickly at wholesale prices and then reselling them slowly at retail prices. The resulting profits are significant, and they can easily afford to finance the properties while they wait for the buyers to close and pay them their profits.

There is a story about a young boy who watched a farmer growing and selling watermelons from his field. One day the boy approached the farmer and inquired about the prices on several melons. The large ripe melons were $3, but one much smaller melon was only $1. The boy gave the farmer a dollar and told him he'd take the small one. The farmer tried to explain that it was not ready to pick yet, and the boy said that was fine, he'd come back in two weeks and get it.

My friends in California understand that if you wait to harvest your houses until they ripen, there is much more money to be made. Some investors buy a house and then try to sell it immediately. Often they make only a small profit, and sometimes they lose. My friends never lose, as they allow buyers to move into the house today and to pay for it when they can afford to buy it. This rent-to-own plan helps buyers to get into a house right away while they get their income, expenses, and credit in good-enough shape to qualify for a loan.

21

Selling a House to a User on Terms

One reason it is hard to sell a house is that new buyers have a hard time obtaining bank financing. When the market is slow and the number of foreclosures increases, lenders tighten their credit requirements. Buyers, who could have qualified under the old rules, can no longer qualify for loans. In addition, the government will often react by passing more laws regulating the lending industry that, while possibly well intended, often will result in fewer options for borrowers. People still want to buy houses but they just can't get a loan.

If you can offer a house with owner financing, you can sell houses when others, who require their borrowers to qualify for a bank loan, cannot. In addition, you can charge a higher price for your house if you offer to finance it at attractive rates.

Building Wealth Buying Foreclosures

Although you will not receive all of your profits today, the profit that you defer will earn you interest or rent. Because you have not received all your money, you can probably defer the taxes on your profit until you receive it using a tax strategy called an "installment sale." Installment sale reporting is available to investors but not dealers who buy and sell property without holding it as an investment. If you hold and rent a house for a year, it should qualify as an investment and for an installment sale.

I sell with short-term financing to buyers who I hope will be able to qualify for a loan in one or two years. Inflation can erode the value of the dollar over time, so I want to get my money back as soon as possible. If you have never sold a house using owner financing, it may sound risky to you. I have sold many houses this way, and find that it is a way to help first-time home buyers get into the market. While my success rate in selling with owner financing is not 100 percent, it is very high for two reasons. First, I get to know the buyers and only sell to those whom I am confident will succeed. My 22 years of experience with Habitat for Humanity has taught me that when homeowners invest more than money into a house, they are more likely to work hard to keep it. Habitat's homeowners help build their own houses. Many of the houses I sell need some work, and when the homeowners invest their labor in that work, it bonds them to the house.

Occasionally an unforeseen event like a job transfer or divorce will cause a home buyer to default. When this happens, I try to work out a happier ending than a foreclosure or an eviction. In more than 30 years of selling houses with owner financing, I have only foreclosed once.

Secondly, I am more flexible than a commercial lender if buyers have a problem. I am able to grant extensions, renegotiate payment schedules, or just let them stay on as tenants if they cannot qualify for a loan eventually.

Qualifying Your Buyers

When lenders qualify potential borrowers, they look at those people's income and expenses and their credit history. When you qualify potential buyers, you may have other criteria, for example, their ability to make repairs on a house that needs them.

Sometimes lenders turn down loan applicants because they have a short-term, solvable credit issue like a new job or have too much debt. Or there could be a credit problem caused by a nonrecurring event like a divorce or accident. These are credit issues that can be overcome with time.

Other borrowers have chronic credit problems because they are poor money managers, experience substance abuse problems, or have poor work habits and can't keep a job. Obviously, if you are going to finance a house for a buyer for a year or two until he or she can qualify for a bank loan, you want someone with a short-term issue, not a chronic problem.

Why a Landlord Has a Different Perspective Than a Seller

Landlords are used to renting houses to tenants and letting them move in with one or two months rent paid in advance, plus a security deposit. If you are a landlord, you are used to sizing up people. You become a quick judge of character and learn to ask probing questions. These skills are valuable if you are going to sell a house and finance it for the buyers. If you are going to allow someone to move into your house with a relatively small down payment, then you need to check out that person before he or she moves in.

How much of a down payment should you charge when selling on terms? The amount of the down payment is negotiable, but before you advertise, you need to set the minimum down payment you will accept.

It should be based both on the market and on the cost of getting your house back if the buyers crash and burn.

·When you simply rent a house, if the tenant does not pay, you can regain possession of the house with an eviction. If you sell someone a house and she does not pay, it is likely to take you longer and cost you more money to regain possession of your house, and to clear the title to the house if you have recorded a document, which gives her an interest in the property. Because of this potential additional cost, you need to collect more money up front when you sell than when you simply rent.

Other than the paperwork, the market in your town will be a determinant of the amount that you can charge when you sell. People who buy from you may not be able to obtain conventional financing. If they have less-than-perfect credit or insufficient income to qualify for a loan, they may be willing to pay you a higher-than-market interest rate but will probably be challenged to come up with the down payment. If buyers have less of a down payment than you have established as a minimum, don't sell them the house but rent it to them and give them some credit toward the purchase price for each payment that they make on time. Charge them more than the market rent, and then give them a generous credit.

Case Study: Selling a House When the Buyer Is Short of the Down Payment

Here are the stats on a house you are looking to sell:

House value	$275,000
Market rent	$1,400
The minimum down payment you would want	$5,000
The down payment your buyers have today	$2,500

> You agree to rent the buyers the house for $1,500 a month ($100 over the market rent) and give them $200 a month credit toward the purchase price of $275,000. At the end of 24 months they will have paid in $2,400 over and above the regular rent. They will have earned $4,800 in credit toward the purchase price. Add that to their $2,500 down payment and you can then enter into an agreement to sell them the house. The credit that they have earned will help them acquire a loan.

Three Different Ways to Sell and Finance a House

The amount of down payment you will want to collect will be influenced by the type of agreement that you use. If you need to pay attorneys and involve the court system to regain your house, you will want to charge more up front.

You have several options when selling and agreeing to finance a house. One is to deed the house to the buyer and carry back a mortgage or deed of trust. Another would be to lease the house with an option to buy, and a third would be to use a land contract or contract for deed.

Knowledge of your local laws and customs will help you decide which will work best in your town. From your standpoint as a seller, you want to use the technique that is the least costly, plus one that gives you the most protection should the deal go sour. Every state has a way to secure real estate debt. Many eastern states use mortgages to secure the debt. Many western states use deeds of trust. In the states that use deeds of trust, the nonjudicial foreclosure period is shorter and often less expensive. If you live in one of those states, financing a purchaser with a small down payment is less risky, as you can get your house back faster if they don't pay you.

In states that use mortgages and require judicial action to foreclose, the process takes longer and is typically more expensive. It would not be advisable to sell a house with a small down payment using a mortgage.

I live in a judicial foreclosure state. Occasionally a buyer will request that we use a mortgage to finance a purchase with a low down payment. I explain that it would take me at least four months to foreclose and the attorney's fees and court costs would be around $3,000. If they are willing to pay an amount equal to four month's rent plus the attorney's fee in addition to the normal down payment, I will agree to record the mortgage. No one wants to make a larger down payment, so we use another type of contract to secure his or her interest and to protect my interest.

Selling Using a Contract Instead of Recording a Mortgage or Trust Deed

Two commonly used contracts allow a buyer with a small down payment to begin acquiring equity in a property. They are lease option contracts and agreements for deed.

A lease option contract combines the features of a lease, which allows the tenant to occupy a property for a certain amount of time for a stated rent, with an option to buy. The option to buy fixes the purchase price for a certain period of time. Typically the price used is today's retail price. It is negotiable, and it could be set by an appraisal at the time of purchase. Most buyers will want to try to negotiate a price today. If you do set a price, set it for as short a period of time that you can negotiate, and then build in extensions at a slightly higher price. In a soft market, use today's price and then add 5 percent a year to the price if they choose to extend.

Selling a House to a User on Terms

By making your rents competitive and by accepting a relatively low down payment, you can charge a retail price when you sell on a lease option. Most buyers are more concerned with the amount down and the monthly payments than the purchase price. They are never going to write a check for the purchase price. One day they will qualify for a loan, which will have payments in the range of their rent payments. The lease option allows them to get into a house today and build equity.

The seller can command a higher price when he or she offers affordable terms. In a slow market, the cash price on a $275,000 house might be $250,000 or less. By selling on a lease option today and waiting a year or two for a full payoff, a patient seller can both sell more quickly and get a larger profit.

Contracts and Agreements for Deed

In many states, especially throughout the Midwest, contracts for deeds (which are the same as agreements for deeds and contracts for sale) are commonly used to sell property on terms. A contract for deed is a less-expensive alternative to deeding a property to someone and then carrying a mortgage. It is a simple document that can be purchased as a form and then filled in by the seller and buyer.

In some western states, notably California, contracts for deeds are rarely used because termination of the contract may require a judicial foreclosure. A judicial foreclosure would take more time and cost more than a trustee's sale.

In states where a contract for deed is commonly used, they provide a simple way for buyers and sellers to enter into an agreement with terms. As the name of the instrument states, it is a contract for a deed, so the deed is not transferred to the buyers until they have completed paying for the property.

Cautions about Using Contracts and Lease Options

There is a risk to using a contract for deed or lease option, especially if you are the buyer. If the seller has financial problems and cannot make the loan payments, the lender can foreclose and wipe out a buyer's interest under either type of contract. Another risk is that if judgments are recorded against the seller (as the title to the property is still in that person's name), the judgment will attach the property, putting the buyers' equity in jeopardy.

One solution that offers some protection is to have a third-party trustee hold title to the house that is being sold. Title-holding trusts, often known as land trusts, are commonly used to have a third party hold title as trustee for the seller. If a trustee holds title, judgments against the seller would not attach. There would still be the risk of foreclosure.

Selling Properties That Need Work in As-Is Condition

When you find yourself with a house that needs major repairs or remodeling, you are faced with a choice. You can spend a significant amount of time and money making the repairs. Or you can sell it for less money immediately in as-is condition.

I have tried both and found that selling in as-is condition is often faster and more profitable than trying to make repairs. Unless you are able to do most of the work needed yourself (and enjoy it), it is hard to just recover your costs of making repairs, much less make a profit. Many home buyers are willing to invest sweat equity in a house if they think that they are getting a bargain and if the financing is affordable.

Another factor is that you can sell a house that needs a lot of work to buyers with a very small down payment without much risk. Require them to make the repairs before they move in (or they may never make them).

Case Study: Disaster House Sold to Loving Family

I purchased a house in foreclosure from owners who had abandoned it a year before. It had been vacant and was both vandalized and in need of a new kitchen, baths, and flooring, and it had significant wall and ceiling damage. My estimated cost to make the needed repairs was $40,000. Before I started the work, a family approached me who liked the location and was willing to take on a project. I asked family members specific questions about their experience fixing up houses and discovered that they had both the skills and other resources necessary to bring this house back. I agreed to sell it to them for $100 down if they would take it in as-is condition, acknowledging that it needed lots of work. (I listed the needed repairs.) I gave them a one-year lease with an option to buy the house. They were successful in turning the house around, and within the year were able to refinance the house and pay me off. They bought a house at a bargain price with only $100 down and made a significant profit for their work. I made an easy $30,000 profit without investing more time and money. If I had invested the additional $40,000 needed to make the repairs, I would have had to sell the house for much more money, and would have been nervous about selling a newly remodeled house for a small down payment. This would have made the house harder to sell and I would have had to wait longer to get my money back.

Selling Dream Homes to Homeowners Is the Best Way to Cash Out

You want to sell to homeowners looking for their dream home. You may not think that a house needing work in a less-than-perfect part of town is someone's dream home, but you are wrong. Every house is someone's dream home. If you are living in a one-bedroom trailer with a leaking roof, a small two-bedroom house with a good roof is your dream home.

Many of us take homeownership for granted because we have owned homes for years and probably our parents owned their home. Tens of millions of families have never owned a home. Others have owned and then lost a home. These families are candidates for the home you are selling, if you will help them with financing.

Buyers will pay your high retail prices when you agree to help them with financing. This will make a considerable difference in your net profit.

Comparison of Selling for Cash and Selling on Terms

Here's how selling for cash and selling for terms typically plays out.

	Cash Sale	Terms Sale
House value	$225,000	$225,000
Probable sales price	$210,000	$225,000
Commission	$12,600	0
Repairs	$1,500	0
Probable net	$195,900	$225,000
Plus: Interest Collected over Three Years with Owner Financing		@ 6% on $220,000: $39,600

While you have to wait for your profits, depending on your alternatives, it may be worth the wait. In the next chapter you will learn how to recover your cash sooner by allowing an investor to share profits with you.

Case Study: Showing Buyers the Wisdom of Investing in a Home Instead of a Car

Automobile companies have done a tremendous job marketing cars, and lenders and insurance companies have made it easy for anyone to own one. Anybody can get financing. If you can't qualify for a new car loan, there are many "buy here, pay here" car dealers who will finance you.

Most people never calculate what their car costs them, but for many it's a choice between buying a new car and buying a house. Here is a conservative comparison of the cost of a $20,000 car and a $200,000 house over a five-year period. Show this to your potential buyers, or put together an example with numbers from your town.

A $20,000 car has payments of $300 a month and is worth less each month.

A $200,000 house has payments of $1,200 a month and is worth more each month.

That's 10 times the value for only four times the cost.

Five years later the house may be worth $250,000, and your loan payments stay the same as long as you live there. Five years later, the car will be worth $10,000 or less, and when you buy another car, your payments will be higher.

A wise family will drive an older paid-for car so that they can afford to buy a house as soon as they can.

22

Selling the House to an Investor

Although selling to an investor may not be your first choice when you buy a house, it is always an option. During boom times the multitudes begin buying property, so "investors" abound. Many of these boom investors are really speculators, buying in anticipation of short-term profits. When the boom ends, they disappear.

In a flat or declining market, only investors with long-term profit motives buy, because they know the big profits will come from holding until the market reverses. These investors want to buy at a price that gives them a return while they hold and a considerable profit when they sell. They often have the ability to finance what they buy even when others can't borrow. There are always investors. Even on the darkest day of the deepest depression, not everybody is broke.

You have several choices when selling to an investor. I use them all successfully, and I've made many financial friends by sharing profits. A financial friend may have only one thing in common with you: your mutual profit. That one thing can be a powerful bond. If you are just selling outright to an investor and have no further connection to him, then that one thing can be enough. If you plan to own property together, then you want more in common. You'll need to share values like honesty and integrity, plus an agreed-upon profit or holding period. (I prefer holding until a property doubles in value rather than setting a time to sell.)

Many people with a lot of money to invest are not interested in managing property. They are trying to make a better return than the bank will pay them, and they don't want to take a chance of losing in the stock market. Their money is "lazy money," but it's "smart lazy money."

An investor who has earned and saved her money is by far a smarter and easier-to-deal-with investor than someone who has inherited it or won the lottery. Someone who has accumulated her fortune over time understands the relationship between time and money, and is willing to keep her money invested and compounding.

Sell It All for a Profit

Although an owner-occupant will pay you more for his or her dream home than an investor will, an investor may buy something in a week, whereas you may have to wait patiently for the right home buyer to fall in love.

Investors are less fickle, less emotional: In short, it is easier to do business with them. I buy regularly from others who find good deals but who cannot afford them. They choose to sell to me at a wholesale price and take a small profit rather than waiting for a larger profit. A good buyer who sells to another investor and averages a profit of $5,000 per house can make a decent living. The investor may make $30,000 to $50,000 on the same house by renting the house, holding it for a year or two, and then selling it to a user at a retail price on terms.

There are options other than just selling for a small, quick profit.

Sell It, Let the Investor Finance It, Then Own It Together

One of my first investors had a limited amount of cash to invest, but he had great credit. When I found a property that we could buy at a great price, my investor would contract to buy it, subject to getting a loan for most of the purchase price. Although I don't like going to banks to borrow money to buy property, it does not bother me to have an investor borrow from the bank.

After the investor closed on the purchase and the loan, he would then deed me one-half interest in the property and I would give him a note for one-half the amount he paid for the down payment and closing costs.

Case Study: Investor Uses Credit to Buy

Here's one typical example of how an investor uses credit to buy:

House value	$250,000
Purchase price	$200,000
New bank loan	$160,000
Investor cash invested	$40,000
My note to the investor	$20,000

When we sell, the investor will receive the $20,000 payment on the note, plus, because he owns one-half interest in the house, he will receive half the profits. It is important to use this strategy when you can borrow on terms that the income from the property will repay. You do not want to call an investor and ask him for more money each month.

Find a Lease Option Buyer, Then Sell the Investor the House

Using the same house as an example, suppose that you had a lease option buyer who would pay $250,000 for the house with a $4,000 down payment and monthly payments of $1,500. You could then look for an investor who would close on the house, purchase at the $200,000 price, and then split the profits with you on the lease option sale. You could let the investor have the $1,500-a-month income (which he could use to repay a loan, if he borrowed to buy the house) and then split the $50,000 profit when the buyer closed on the option purchase.

You could either split the option payment with the investor or agree that you would receive the option payment and he would keep the monthly payments.

If the lease option buyer did not close, you could give him an extension at a slightly higher price, say $260,000. If you determine that he is unlikely to be able to close, even with the extension, then look for another buyer. In a soft market I have sold the same house several times. Each time I was able to raise the price, and each time I collected another down payment.

Selling the House to an Investor

You are valuable to the investor because you found a house that you can buy at a bargain price and then you found a buyer at a retail price. The investor is taking little risk, as he is buying a house 20 percent below the market and has no work to do.

It is a good deal for you because you make a profit on a deal that you might not be able to buy without the investor.

23

Accelerating Your Plan for Building Wealth

As explained in my first two books, *Building Wealth One House at a Time* and *Building Real Estate Wealth in a Changing Market*, when you buy steadily in all types of markets, you can accumulate a portfolio of houses that can provide you with a growing net worth and an ever-increasing income stream.

Buying one house a year until the first house doubles in value can result in annual income greater than the value of the first house you purchased.

Here is an example of the results of buying one house a year and holding each one until the first one doubles in value. The length of time it will take to double depends on your market plus your ability to buy below the market. This example assumes that you buy 10 percent below the market and on the average year the houses will appreciate at a 5 percent rate. These are both conservative assumptions. You can buy houses at deeper discounts, and you can buy in neighborhoods that appreciate above the average in your town.

Beginning of Year	Original House Value, $	Original Purchase Price, $	House Value End of Year 14
1	200,000	180,000	400,000
2	210,000	189,000	400,000
3	221,000	198,000	400,000
4	232,000	208,000	400,000
5	244,000	219,000	400,000
6	255,000	230,000	400,000
7	268,000	241,000	400,000
8	281,000	253,000	400,000
9	295,000	265,000	400,000
10	310,000	279,000	400,000
11	325,000	292,000	400,000
12	342,000	308,000	400,000
13	359,000	323,000	400,000
14	377,000	339,000	400,000
	Totals	$3,524,000	$5,600,000
		Gross Profit	$2,076,000
Equity (total values less approximate loan values)			$2,780,800

At the end of year 14, you will own a portfolio of houses that produce significant cash flow and that are paying off their own debt at an increasing pace.

You would own a real estate portfolio that would increase in value $280,000 (5 percent of $5.6 million) in an average year. Plus it would pay off about $100 a day in debt and produce between $5,000 and $10,000 a month in cash flow, depending on your management skills.

You can't get too good at management. Every little thing you learn about selecting and training tenants will make you dollars every month for the rest of your life. Study landlording and become a great landlord. It pays very well. I highly recommend that you study my one-day course on managing houses titled "Positive Landlording" to develop the skills that you need to maximize your rental income.

Nine Ways to Accelerate Your Investment Program

1. *Buy more often.* Although buying one house a year will make you wealthy, it will take time. If you are a quick study and a hard worker, you can buy more than one house a year. Your risk increases somewhat, but you can offset risk with knowledge and skills. If you are a smart manager and can keep your properties full of good tenants, then moving faster is an option that will multiply your profits. Buy one house, rent it, then buy another.

2. *Buy aggressively in a down market.* Real estate markets cycle regularly, so you can expect a buying opportunity at least once a decade or so. When you recognize and are ready for a buying opportunity, buy at much larger discounts (30 to 50 percent) and then hold the property until the market takes off again. People who buy in a hot market pay retail and hope that the property will continue to appreciate. Buying at a significant discount in a down market is a safe and smart strategy.

Building Wealth Buying Foreclosures

3. *When markets are depressed, lenders are too.* A lender in trouble will make you a better-than-market deal on both interest rates and payments when you buy. Negotiate hard when buying property that lenders own, or when you are taking over an existing loan. They are anxious to get rid of property or not to foreclose on any more. It's time to buy and borrow at great rates!

4. *In a down market, you can often buy a property with a very small down payment.* As you are not trying to qualify for a new loan, you can buy by making one or two back payments and taking over an existing loan. Lenders will often agree to add the back payment to the loan balance, so you can actually buy with nothing down, the title of one of my students, Robert Allen's book *Nothing Down*, (Simon and Schuster, 1981). This gives you the ability to buy a number of properties in a short time with only a little cash. When you buy with a small down payment, the potential return on your money is phenomenal. Buying a $180,000 house for $140,000 with $2,000 down (a real deal) produces a "going-in profit" of 20 times your investment, and it's real. Learn to buy and negotiate with lenders and you can make returns so good to tell your friends about.

5. *Buy in only the best areas of your town.* When a market is hot, prices will flare in the most desirable areas of your town. When the market is cold, properties in many of these areas will dramatically drop in value as the speculators bail out. If you can buy in better areas, you will reap larger profits when the market reverses. Do research into which areas faired the best in the last boom period, and try to buy a few houses at deep discounts in those areas when the market is down.

6. *Buy only on terms that fit your plan.* If your plan is to buy only properties that you can rent for more than the loan payments you are making, establish that as your policy and make offers that will allow

you to accomplish your goals. If your plan is not to invest more than $5,000 in any one property, then make offers that ask lenders and sellers to finance the rest. If you buy a property that has cash flow you don't like, the problem is not the property, it is your offer.

7. *When you sell, sell to a user or buyer who wants your property and who will pay you a retail price (or even higher, if the terms are good).* Don't wholesale to other investors. Have a plan that allows you to hold a house long enough to sell it for a large profit in the next up market.

8. *Improve your cash flow by being smart when you pay off debt.* When you sell a house, try to pay off a debt you owe that will dramatically increase your cash flow. Often it will be a short-term loan, a high-interest-rate loan, or maybe a private loan that you can pay off for less than face value. Study these examples.

	Balance	Payments	Interest Rate
Loan 1	$80,000	$1,200	8%
Loan 2	$60,000	$250	5%

Loan 1 is to a homeowner who has sold you a house in return for you taking over his existing $80,000 loan at 8 percent interest and agreeing to pay him $250 a month on the balance for 10 years, with the balance due in full in 10 years. The seller has called you and said that he would take $25,000 today as payment in full for his note as he has the opportunity to buy another property. You decide to pay the seller the $25,000, saving $250 a month and $35,000.

These opportunities are common when one is dealing with sellers who finance. They are rare with commercial lenders, but they do occasionally occur.

9. *Always ask for a discount when paying off a loan.* If you ask for and get a discount when you pay off any debt, it will accelerate your program. Make this a habit. I have friends who ask for discounts when they buy milk at the grocery store, and they occasionally get it. I think that's a little silly, but asking for a $5,000 or $10,000 or $50,000 discount when you pay off a loan is not silly, it is profitable negotiation at the highest level.

Increasing Your Income by Selectively Selling

Unless you want to die with an awful lot of equity, you could begin selling a house every so often to increase your spendable income. Another advantage of selling is that you can get rid of the houses that cause you the most trouble. Some houses attract great tenants, and others, not so great ones. If the finances make sense, sell off the ones that give you the most trouble first. Once a year you could sell a house and replace it with a newer house that you could buy on good terms.

Suppose that in year 15 you could sell the house you bought in year 1 for $400,000. At that time you would owe approximately $115,000 on the loan, leaving a gross profit of about $285,000.

Sell first house you bought	$400,000
Pay off loan	$115,000
Net before taxes	$285,000

This house you bought for less than $200,000 has now made you a profit of $285,000 plus the rent you have collected for the last 14 years.

You could now just pay any tax due and spend the rest, but a better plan would be to take part of these proceeds and purchase another investment house, taking advantage of the ability to reinvest tax free under Section 1031 of the Internal Revenue Code.

Using Part of the Sales Proceeds to Buy a Replacement House

House sale proceeds	$400,000
Pay off loan	$115,000
Net before taxes	$285,000
Purchase another investment property	$85,000
Balance left subject to taxes	$200,000

After years of experience buying investment properties, your skill level will be at a peak, and you will be able to buy a property far below the market and on great terms so that it will produce cash flow from day one.

Another Option: Sell to Produce Long-Term Income

An alternative would be to sell house number 1 on terms and enjoy the income and interest earned on your profit.

If you did, house number 1 could produce cash flow of approximately $25,400 a year, assuming that you can charge a 9 percent interest rate when you sell. If rates are much lower, you would be wiser to sell for cash, as prices will be high when interest rates are very low. In the following example the property has an existing loan balance with payments of $1,020 a month.

Selling on Terms

Sales price	$400,000
Down payment	$10,000
Balance due	$390,000 payable over 30 years at 9 percent interest with payments of $3,138 less $1,020-a-month payment on the first nets $2,118 a month, or $25,416 a year

Paying Taxes Only on Money You Receive That Year

When you sell an investment property and finance it for the buyer, you are able to pay taxes on your profits as you receive them, taking advantage of "installment sale" reporting. This gives you the additional advantage of earning interest on all of your profit, rather than paying a tax and then just earning interest on what's left. Check with your Certified Public Accountant, as tax laws are constantly changing.

Sell for all cash and net before taxes	$285,000
Pay 15 percent in taxes	$42,750
Amount you have to invest or spend	$242,250

Compare the $25,416 annual income to the $280,000 (both before tax) income you could receive from selling for cash, and decide which is best for you and your family.

Your Legacy

If your heirs are good managers, then inheriting a portfolio of well-located properties would be a great benefit. If they are not good money or property managers, then instead of leaving them houses to manage, selling the houses and creating a number of mortgages with a virtually guaranteed long-term income stream may be a wiser strategy.

You could place the houses in a trust, which could then sell them and collect the mortgages. The trustee would then distribute the income to you during your life and to your heirs afterward. You could serve as the trustee and name a successor trustee who would take over if you were unable to serve as one. The successor trustee can be a family member or trusted friend with the skills needed to manage the assets, or it can be an institution like a bank or trust company.

If you have heirs, chances are they all have different personalities and talents. If so, you could leave houses to the heir with management talent and leave mortgages to the others.

24

If You Find Yourself in Trouble

As an investor, you may find it easy to buy property and sometimes too easy to borrow money. Buying a lot of property is not necessarily the path to making a lot of money. For example, one young investor bought 15 houses in one year, but he subsequently lost them because he bought beyond his ability to manage them.

If It Seems Easy, You May Be Doing It Wrong

As the investor who bought 15 houses in one year learned, just buying houses does not guarantee you a profit. In a down market, people will line up to sell you their houses if you will take over their loans. It's a temptation you would be wise to resist.

Building Wealth Buying Foreclosures

Owning a number of empty houses will eat up a lot of cash in short order. Unfortunately, houses that you can buy with nothing down often have large payments. Many new landlords have grown old trying to rent a house for an amount that will cover the mortgage payments when the market rent would be $400 lower.

Another trap is buying with short-term financing in a market where interest rates are rising. Unfortunately, I fell in this trap early in my career. I found that a lot of sellers would let me take over their payments and give them a five-year note for their equity.

Unfortunately, five years later, interest rates had doubled.

It's hard to borrow and harder to sell when interest rates are high. Sometimes when you are going in the wrong direction you don't realize it until its too late. There are some warning signs that might alert you that you are getting in trouble. Check yourself against this list:

1. You own empty properties.
2. You are borrowing money to pay interest.
3. You have tenants who are behind in their rent.
4. You cannot afford to maintain your properties.
5. You are not paying your bills on time.
6. You avoid thinking about some of your empty properties.
7. You are not sleeping well.

If one or two of these signals are present, stop buying and take steps to improve your financial situation. If more than two are applicable to your situation, then this is your wake-up call! You are heading the wrong way and need to make some changes.

Solutions

If you own several empty properties, take a day and really check out your competition. Drive five blocks in every direction from your properties and stop and look at every house for sale or for rent. If these homes are comparable to yours, call the owners and get the rent and deposit or the asking price and terms. Write all of this down so you have addresses, phone numbers, and prices or rents. You can get on your computer on a slow day and look up who owns them and what they paid for them. You may want to follow up and try to buy one or more of them.

You now know your competition and can beat them. Recognize that your potential tenants are doing about the same exercise before they rent. Now do two things: Make your house look the best from the street, and price it at the bottom of the range. Hire someone who needs the work to spend a day in the yard making it look great. Paint the front door, the mailbox post, and the garage door, if they need it. Put a good-looking sign in the yard. It does not have to be an expensive sign, but buy a new sign and you will get more calls.

Now, one more important thing that will make your house rent the fastest: Answer the phone when they call. If you answer the phone and talk to prospective tenants, you may be the only landlord who they can actually get on the phone. The rest will get a recording. This step is even more important if you are trying to sell a house. Especially in a slow market you want to talk to every potential buyer. If they don't buy this house, you may have another or find another next week. Get their names, numbers, and what they want.

If you are borrowing money to pay interest, then you have to ask a couple of questions. Are you likely to be able to continue to borrow for the foreseeable future? In a tightening credit market, banks often cancel lines of credit. If your plan is to borrow on an unsecured line of credit to fund your negative cash flow, it could hit a snag if the bank refuses to loan you more money.

The other question: Is your market improving? If it is not, maybe you are better off selling today for a loss rather than feeding a losing property that is declining in value.

Suppose your choice is selling for a $50,000 loss or continuing to hold and lose $2,000 a month. If you sell and take the loss, you are now free to go out and buy something else at a discount and on terms that you can afford. If you continue to hold and sell for $25,000 more in another year, you are not really ahead, as you lost a year to shop for a better property.

If you have tenants who are behind in their rent, call them in and ask them (husband and wife or all occupants) some pointed questions about their current employment and expenses. By calling a meeting, you make a point that this situation is serious. Form a plan where they agree from this point forward to pay a certain amount on time; then have them sign a letter stating the agreement.

A couple of options are available to you. If the tenants just cannot get their act together to pay the full rent once a month and you would like to keep them as tenants, then you could have them begin to pay you once a week (or every two weeks coinciding with their pay period) at a rate equal to one-fourth (or one-half) of their monthly rental. Explain and write down that this is a change from a once-a-month payment schedule, and that payment is due every Friday (or every other Friday). By paying every week or two weeks, they will actually pay more rent than they would once a month (since there are 4.3 weeks in an average month). You will have to do more work, depositing twice or four times a month. Explain to them if they can get where they could once again pay monthly it would save them a few dollars each month.

The second option would be to reduce the tenants' rent. Rather than just giving them a discount, you could trade out some work you need at the house for the reduction in rent. Perhaps they could do some yardwork or simple painting. This arrangement would allow them to save face and let you keep good tenants in your house in a slow rental market.

If the tenants have had a major change in their lives and cannot afford to stay in your house, stop the bleeding and agree on a date that they will leave the house. Offer them some of their deposit back if they will leave it clean and on time. You might offer them a bonus if you are able to rent the house to someone else before they move.

If you cannot afford to maintain your properties, you need to ask if the problem is high maintenance costs or a shortage of cash flow. Sometimes it is one or two properties that take a disproportionate share of the cash flow. If you can identify a property that costs much more than others to maintain, sell it with a lease option at your first chance.

If a shortage of cash flow is the problem, you may own more properties than you can afford. Can you sell one and raise enough cash to give you a cushion? Can you sell a half-interest in one of your houses to a passive investor? If you can, you don't have to wait for a tenant to move out before you sell. Another cause of low cash flow is high-cost financing. If you are going to sell a property, look at your loans and try to get rid of the one with the highest payments.

If you are not paying your bills on time, review your last year's income and expenses to analyze where you are spending your money on an annual basis. You tax return will show an accurate account reported on your Schedule E. When you begin paying your service people late, two things might happen: their response time might be slower and their bills might be higher. It's to your advantage to be able to pay on time and tell your providers that you want good service and a good price, and that you will pay them promptly for their work.

If you have a number of properties, you can increase your cash flow in a flat market by selling houses to your existing tenants or to new tenants using a lease option. With a lease option, you can collect an option fee up front, or charge higher-than-market rent, or both, in return for giving your tenants the right to buy at today's price. When prices are stable, you are not giving away much by using this strategy. Keep your option term relatively short, three years or less, to encourage your tenants to buy before the market gets hot again. Then you will have the resources to buy back in.

Avoiding thinking about some of your empty properties; denial is a common response when every day brings the same results. Although it is hard to stay positive when there is little activity, you can actually make something happen if you will keep trying different approaches to market a property. If a newspaper ad is not producing results, try holding open houses or walking door to door with flyers that describe the house. Tell everyone with whom you do business about your house for sale or rent. Carry flyers with you and answer your phone.

When there is 6 percent unemployment, 94 percent are still working. When 60 percent of the families in your town own their home, 40 percent still want a house. Price your house competitively, and market it aggressively.

If you are not sleeping well, when you wake up in the middle of the night write down the problem that is bothering you. The next morning, first determine if the problem is a big one or a little one. If it's a little one, like a tenant not paying the rent, follow my advice above and solve the problem. If it's a big one, for example you owe somebody $50,000 next month and know that you can't pay him, go tell him now. It will then become his problem as well as yours and you can work together to solve it. Most problems can be solved if you just confront them. Don't lose sleep over a problem; confront it. Often the solution is easier than you think.

25

If You Can't Buy
Their House

Here are some tips that you can give homeowners in trouble if you can't or don't want to buy their house. These ideas may help them save their home and make you a new friend. Wealth is more than money, it's the friends you make and the good you do for others.

Save Your Home: How to Avoid a Foreclosure and Eventually Pay Off Your Debt

Act Today—Don't Be Paralyzed by Guilt or Debt!

Whether you are just about to lose your home or the foreclosure is weeks away, there is something that you can do. Many homeowners in trouble simply refuse to admit that they have a problem. If you can't make your house payment, or if you are struggling to pay other bills, you have a problem and need to deal with it.

Your creditors and lenders may not seem sympathetic, but they do want to be paid and are willing to be part of the solution, if you will make them an offer.

Five Reasons to Do Something Today

1. *Your credit is further damaged every day that you wait.* When you get further behind on your payments, your borrowing options become very limited. Any lender can check your credit nearly instantly. If you are late paying all of your bills, obtaining a debt consolidation loan or refinancing other loans will become more and more difficult.

2. *The longer you wait, the less you are likely to receive when you sell.* When the real estate market is in a slump, waiting longer will result in fewer buyers and lower offers. In addition, once a notice of a foreclosure sale is published, the whole world knows that you are under pressure to sell and the offers will be even lower. Often the first offer you get is the best offer.

3. *It often takes several days to contact the lender and negotiate a deal.* If you wait until the day before your foreclosure sale to call your lender, chances are she will not be able to help you. If you call her when you are only one month behind, you have several weeks to renegotiate your loan terms or agree on a workout plan. Typically you will have to go through at least two steps to get any modification of your loan approved. During a recent renegotiation, I talked to two different bank officials several times each over a period of two weeks before reaching an agreement.

4. *If your loan is being foreclosed through a judicial process, then once a lawyer becomes involved, you will be responsible for paying*

his expenses. Your loan documents allow the lender to hire an attorney and to charge you the costs.

5. *The faster you solve your house problem, the faster you can get back on track to financial solvency and then on to financial independence.* It is hard to be positive about your future when the wolf is at your door. Get rid of the wolf, even at a loss. You will then be in better shape to buy another property at a bargain price. The day you renegotiate or shed the debt that you cannot repay is the day your credit will begin to improve.

Learning about the Foreclosure Process in Your State

Different states have different foreclosure procedures. If you are in a state that uses judicial foreclosure, you will generally have more time between the time you stop making payments and the day of the foreclosure sale. In states that use a nonjudicial trustees' foreclosure, you will receive a notice of default and then have a period of time to cure the default before the sale. After the sale, there is no right to redeem your property. If you signed a mortgage when you borrowed, your lender must use a judicial foreclosure. If you signed a deed of trust, they will hold a trustees' sale. You can search on the Internet for information about the foreclosure process in your state. Some of the Internet sites will be trying to sell you a service or lend you money. Be wary.

The Timeline

If you are behind on your loan payments, you should begin receiving mail from your lenders first scolding you and later on encouraging you to work something out. If you do not respond or cannot work out an arrangement with the lender, then the lender will file an action to foreclose or to hold a trustees' sale. Right up until the day of that sale, you have the ability to reinstate your loan or to negotiate some settlement with the lender.

Some states that use the judicial foreclosure process allow homeowners to redeem their property, even after the foreclosure sale. To redeem, the homeowners must pay off all the debt plus any fees associated with the foreclosure.

The Seven Stages of Losing Your House

1. You buy and borrow.
2. You realize that you are going to miss a payment.
3. You miss the payment.
4. You get a notice from the lender.
5. Action to foreclose is filed.
6. A notice of sale is published.
7. A sale occurs.

Also, a redemption period occurs (in some states).

Avoiding Bad Loan and Predatory Lenders

Some lenders specialize in lending to homeowners who are in financial trouble. Borrowing more from these lenders not only gets you deeper in debt but also makes the loans harder to pay. My friend and fellow instructor, Jack Miller describes debt consolidation loans as when you "take several smaller, hard-to-pay loans and rolling them into one big impossible-to-pay loan."

Every time you borrow money, there are additional charges that make your debt bigger. Borrowers are often fooled by teaser interest rates that jump to a much higher rate if you are even one day late on your payments. If you are having trouble paying today, rather than getting a new loan, renegotiate with your existing lenders.

Loaning to Own

Some lenders are in the "loan-to-own" business. When they make you a loan, they hope that you will default so that they can get your house for the amount of their loan. Other lenders charge high up-front fees to a borrower to make a loan and then immediately sell the loan. They don't want your house, they just want their big fees.

There are both federal and state laws that regulate lending to homeowners in financial distress and other predatory lending. Unfortunately, some lenders are not experts on these relatively new laws. Many small lenders have few assets, so they play fast and loose. Search the Internet for laws about predatory lending and learn your rights before you borrow.

Assessing Your Current Situation

It's hard to be objective and totally rational when you are making personal financial decisions. It's easier to give friends advice about how to solve their problems than to give yourself advice. You are removed emotionally from your friends' problems, but you can't be totally unemotional about your own situation.

Many financial decisions are made for emotional reasons. If you are under stress, you may think that you are in worse shape than you really are. This section will help you objectively assess your current condition.

Do you currently have enough income to pay your bills? If so, you might be able to get each of your creditors to either forgive your back payments or add your back payments to your account if you can show them that you are able to keep them current.

If you don't have enough money to pay your bills, ask yourself if there are any bills that you can eliminate.

Three Ways to Dramatically Improve Your Cash Flow

1. Cut Your Expenses

Cut Your Car Expenses

Car expenses are a major outflow. I drove an old mail jeep I bought for next to nothing until I could afford to pay cash for a better car. It only had one seat, so I was rarely asked to drive anywhere. If you are struggling financially, consider downsizing your means of transportation, all the way down to a bicycle, if you can. Eliminating all the expenses your car produces can make a major swing in your cash flow.

Start Eating In

Eating out and buying prepared food costs several times what it cost to buy and prepare your own food. If you don't cook, learn. It's a good survival skill. Shop only once a week and make a list of what you need before you go. Study the store flyer and buy things on sale. My grandmother and I would shop only on Thursday and would go to three different grocery stores, buying only what was on sale at each store. She raised four boys during the Depression and could make a soup or stew with just a little meat that was a healthy and tasty meal. Occasionally take yourself and family out to a meal, and it will be a real treat.

If You Can't Buy Their House

Tighten Up on Your Other Expenses

Another significant drain on cash flow is your utility bill. Learn all you can about ways to save money by setting your thermostat a little higher or lower, checking to make sure no plumbing is leaking. A little insulation or weather stripping can do a lot to keep cold air in or out. Although many now see air conditioning as a necessity, it was a rarity a generation ago, so you can live without it. Make it a game to see how much you can save compared to the same month a year ago.

If you buy most things either with a credit card or by writing a check, go through your old bills or last year's check register and look at every dollar you spent. Now write down the things you wish you had not bought. Were any of them impulse buys, things that seemed like a good idea at the time but that you regretted later?

Learn from your past, and don't repeat your mistakes this year. If you are a smart buyer, not an impulse buyer, you can save one-third or more of all that you spend.

2. Increase Your Income

It's easier and faster to cut expenses than to increase your cash flow, but by doing both you can make a big change in your financial situation. Work more hours. If 40 hours a week won't pay the bills, either try to work more hours on your current job or take on another job. Many work two nearly full-time jobs. I just sold a house to a single mom with six children: She works two jobs.

When you are working, you are not spending. Sometimes you can even eat free. Some very successful people I know used to work a full-time day job and then work another job at night. Nearly every successful business owner at one time worked 16 hours a day or more to get his or her business started. It was a sacrifice being away from the family for long hours, but these people did what they had to do to pay the bills.

Building Wealth Buying Foreclosures

When I started in business, I not only worked long hours, I shared every expense that I could. I sublet my office to two others, and the three of us shared the expense of the rent, secretary's salary, phone bill, and even the copy machine. We all did what we could to minimize our expenses because we had little cash flow.

If you own a house and have an empty room, you could share your house expenses by getting a roommate. In fact, some clever students rent houses with several bedrooms and rent the other bedrooms for enough to live there rent free.

There are endless ways to make extra money from home, from making phone calls for pay to tutoring others in whatever you are good at. I have made a part-time career of teaching others about money. You may have another gift like cooking, or photography, or computers that you could teach others.

3. Stop Paying Interest

Poor people pay interest, rich people collect it. Which do you want to be? Poor people not only pay interest but they pay at a higher rate. When wealthy people borrow, they get the best possible rate, but the poor borrower will pay a high rate. Not fair? Maybe, but you can't change the system, you can only change the way you acquire things. Set a goal to first stop paying interest, and then to become an investor so that you can start collecting it.

The first step in not paying interest is to stop borrowing. If you have balances on your credit card and are paying interest, lock them away (or cut them up). If you have a big car loan, do what you need to do to get rid of the car and the loan, then get transportation you can afford to buy for cash. To get rid of your debt, target the smallest one and pay it off. As soon as you pay off the smallest one, target the next smallest one and pay it off until you are out of short-term debt.

If You Can't Buy Their House

You can use this strategy to pay off all of your debt. Owning your home free and clear will give you a sense of satisfaction and accomplishment for the rest of your life.

Debt is not necessarily a bad thing. Investment real estate is often financed. The key is not to borrow more than the property's income can repay.

Serious Questions about Your House Today

What is your house worth today? You don't need an appraisal. You can get online on your local property appraiser's Web site and check what other properties have sold for in your neighborhood this year. As an alternative, call Realtors who have property for sale in your neighborhood and ask them for a list of recent sales.

If you did not own your house, would you buy it again today? If your answer is yes, but at a lower price, then you should try to keep the house but ask the lender to rewrite your loan for a longer term or at a lower interest rate, to lower your payment.

Why did you buy it? Is the reason that you bought it important enough to fight to keep it? If so, fight! If not, if the house is a tremendous burden, offer to deed it to the lender in lieu of a foreclosure.

Can you afford to keep it with the income and other expenses that you have today? Are you willing to work more or to sublet part of your house to increase your income to a level (or cut other expenses) that will allow you to keep the house?

Communicating with the Lender

Keep good records of your payments and correspondence with the lender. You might assume that an institutional lender would keep perfect records and never make a mistake. But you would be wrong. People at the bank are entering your payments, and any time people are involved, mistakes are made.

You probably pay your payments with a check, or the bank is making direct withdrawals from your account. Either way, you should be able to reconstruct from your bank statements how much and when you paid the bank.

Take the time to review your payment history before you contact the lender. If you begin making partial payments, or make a lump-sum payment to bring the loan current, keep careful records. Sometimes a borrower will make two or more payments with one check and the lender will give him credit for one month's payment and use the rest to pay down the principal.

If you are behind in your payments, the lender will typically write you and give you a number to call regarding your account. Much of your communication is likely to be over the telephone. If you are able to reach an agreement to modify your payments, the lender typically will mail or fax you a copy of the agreement with the terms spelled out. Make a copy of this agreement or scan it, and put it someplace safe.

Six Things Lenders Will Do to Help You

1. *Forgive late fees.* This is a cheap and easy way for the lenders to help you get current again. Hopefully, you have contacted the lenders before they have spent money on attorney's fees, which are harder to get forgiven.

2. *Forgive back interest.* If you are struggling to make your payments but can show that with a fresh start you can make it, then the lenders will go a step further and forgive the accrued interest on your loan.

3. *If you are several payments behind and cannot afford to make up your back payments, then they can agree to add your back payments to the amount of your loan, which will lengthen the terms on your loan.*

4. *If your income has dropped and that is the cause of your problems, lenders can agree to a lower interest rate and a lower monthly payment.*

5. *If you cannot make the payments but have a buyer willing to pay you less than what you owe on the house, they can accept a lower amount for their loan.* This is commonly called a "short sale." Ask for an agreement that they will not pursue you for the difference between what they were owed and the amount that they collect as part of your deal.

6. *If you cannot make your payments and do not have a buyer, you can offer to deed the house back to the lender.* This is called a "deed in lieu of foreclosure" and is the lenders' last choice other than foreclosure. If you have a second mortgage or other liens against the property, then a lender will not accept the deed, as that lender would then own the property subject to all of the debt.

Things That You Can Do to Help the Lender

When you ask lenders to help you by modifying their loans, they have to be able to document that the only way they are going to be repaid is to modify your loans. They will be looking for documentation from you that proves your case.

If you want your payments reduced, then you need to show proof that your income is not sufficient to make the current payments. Perhaps your payments have adjusted upwards, or maybe your income has dropped.

If you are asking them to accept a short-sale offer, then they are going to want proof that the properties around you are selling for less than what they sold for a year ago.

If you want to deed your house back to the lender, it will want proof that this option is your only one other than bankruptcy. Document that you have no other assets and that your income cannot support the house.

Buying or Renting Another House

If you are able to sell your house, or give it back to the bank, you should be able to negotiate a month to move to give yourself a chance to find another house to move into. Ironically, after you get out from under your old house loan, you become a better credit risk.

Although a banker will not be anxious to make you a new loan for about two years, many landlords and sellers will be willing to rent or sell you a house. If the real estate market is depressed in your town, it's a great time to buy. Look for a landlord who will allow you to rent with an option to buy or for a seller with a vacant house who will sell to you on terms.

Buying using a lease option typically will give you the lowest monthly payments. With a lease option purchase, generally the seller still pays the taxes and insurance. This keeps your payments lower than they would be if you bought the same house, even using owner financing.

The advantage of buying with owner financing is that you can often get a longer term. Your credit is probably damaged, so any chance of a conventional loan in less than two years is remote. If you can negotiate a five-year term or longer with owner financing, it will give you a good chance to get your credit in order and shop for the best long-term loans.

The third option is to find an affordable rental and begin saving your money for the down payment on your next house. The advantage of renting is that you can get a lot of house for less than what it would cost you to buy, and it's safer. If the roof or your furnace fails, you have little or no responsibility. If you can find a long-term rental, you can stay in one house, avoid the costs of moving again, and save up for your next home purchase.

Conclusion

There are always foreclosure opportunities. When the housing market is soft, there are extraordinary opportunities to buy at deeper discounts and on terms that are rarely available in a normal market.

In one year, you might acquire what may take five years in a normal market. Have a buying plan that keeps you from overbuying and becoming a distressed owner yourself. Have a plan, and follow it: Buy the best properties you can afford at deep discounts and on great terms, and enjoy and share the wealth you accumulate.

You can profit from buying foreclosures and help owners in your community who have no other options.

Additional Resources

Jack Miller: www.Cashflowconcepts.com

Peter Fortunato: www.Petefortunato.com

Jay DeCima: www.fixerjay.com

Dyches Boddiford: www.Assets101.com

John Adams: www.Money99.com

Leigh Robinson: www.landlording.com

John T. Reed: www.johntreed.com

Mike Butler: www.Mikebutler.com

Millard Fuller: www.Fullercenter.org

Habitat for Humanity: www.Habitat.org

Appendix

Foreclosure Property Purchase Worksheet

Today's Date: __/__/__ Source of Lead: _____

Property Address: _____

Owners: Name (s):_____

Phone numbers: (____) _____; (____) _____

Best time to call: _____

House Size: Bedrooms ___; Baths ___; Square Feet ___; Lot Size ___

Garage:_____ Basement: _____ Pool: _____ Fenced Yard: _____

Other Features: _____

Personal Property Included with the house: _____

Is Property listed for sale? _____ If so, with whom? _____Phone____

Date of Purchase: ___/___/___ Original Purchase Price $ _____

Assessed Value: _____ Most Current Appraisal $_____ Date:_/__/__

Is it rented?____ If so, how much is the rent $ ____ Deposit? $ _____

Repairs needed: Estimated Cost

_____ $ _____

_____ $ _____

_____ $ _____

Current Loan and Outstanding Lien Balances:

1. $_____ to _____ payable $_____; Interest Rate _____%

2. $_____ to _____ payable $_____; Interest Rate _____%

3. $_____ to _____ payable $_____; Interest Rate _____%

4. $_____ to _____ payable $_____; Interest Rate _____%

Are the payments current? # 1 _____# 2 _____# 3 _____ # 4 _____

Amount of arrearages: # 1 $_____# 2 $_____# 3 $_____ # 4 $_____

Appendix

Contact Information for the lenders:

	Loan Numbers	Phone Numbers	Contact
1.	_____	_____	_____
2.	_____	_____	_____
3.	_____	_____	_____
4.	_____	_____	_____

Results of your contact with the lenders:

1. Renegotiate Payment to $ ____ Reduced Interest to : ____% Other: _____
2. Renegotiate Payment to $ ____ Reduced Interest to : ____% Other: _____
3. Renegotiate Payment to $ ____ Reduced Interest to : ____% Other: _____
4. Renegotiate Payment to $ ____ Reduced Interest to : ____% Other: _____

Other encumbrances: _____

Seller's Stated Reason for Sale: _____

Best Date for seller to close: ____/____/____

Amount Seller is hoping to get for their equity $ _____

Your first offer: _____

Result: _____

Your Second Offer:_____

Result :_____

Notes_____

Appendix

Example of Purchase Money Note Without Interest

Promissory Note

May 1, 2007

For value received, I promise to pay to the order of Molly Smith, at First National Bank and Trust Company, 1600 Main Street, Sarasota, FL 34236, or other such place as the holder of this note shall designate from time to time, the sum of One Hundred Thousand and no/100, ($100,000.00), which note shall be payable One Thousand ($1000.00) Dollars on the first day of June 2007 and a like sum on or before the first of each calendar month thereafter until the full amount of this note shall have been paid. The maker thereof hereby reserves the right to pay any additional amounts on said note at any time and from time to time without interest.

It is agreed that time is of the essence of this note and that in the event of default in the payment of any installment of this note, for a period of thirty (30) days, the holder of the note, at her option, may declare the remainder of said debt due and collectible, and any failure to exercise the said option shall not constitute a waiver of the right to exercise said option in the event of any future default. If any payment of this note is not paid as above set forth and remains unpaid for said period of thirty (30) days, then such payment shall bear interest at the rate of nine (9%) percent per annum until paid. In the event of default of the payment of this note and the same is collected by or through an attorney at law, I agree to pay all costs of collection, including a reasonable attorney's fee. The drawers and endorsers severally waive presentment for payment, protest and notice of protest, and non-payment of this note.

(Signed) John W. Schaub, III   SEAL
John W. Schaub III, Trustee

Appendix

This is a <u>buyer's</u> contract, and gives the buyer more protection

CONTRACT FOR THE PURCHASE OF REAL ESTATE

PARTIES: Buyer   and Buyer's heirs and assigns,
of:
and Seller   and Seller's heirs and assigns,
of:
hereby agree that the Buyer shall buy and that the Seller shall sell the below described real property under the following terms and conditions:

SUBJECT PROPERTY: Address is:
Legally described as:

PURCHASE PRICE AND TERMS:

The full purchase price shall be: $

1. Earnest money deposit to apply to purchase price: $
2. Balance of down payment payable before closing: $
3. Purchase money note: $
4. Total cash due when title transfers: $

PURCHASE MONEY MORTGAGE: Buyer shall execute and deliver Seller a purchase money note secured by a mortgage acceptable to the buyer in recordable form for the agreed upon balance and terms. This note shall be payable without interest in _____monthly payments of $_____ with the first payment due on _____.

CONVEYANCE: Insurable title shall be deeded to the Buyer subject to any liens, restrictions, encumbrances or easements of record, subject to any mortgages (if any) and taxes for the year of closing and subsequent years. The seller will pay for a buyers and mortgagee policy to be delivered to the buyer.

TITLE INSURANCE: Buyer shall have ten days to examine title and at their option purchase title insurance. If seller is providing a purchase money mortgage, then buyer will provide seller with a mortgagee title policy. In the event the title is uninsurable, the seller shall have 120 days to cure the defects that render the title uninsurable. If seller is unable to cure the defects then the buyer shall have the option of taking title in its existing condition or be entitled to a refund of the earnest money deposited with the seller. All obligations and liability on the part of the seller will terminate with the refund of the deposit.

Appendix

TERMITE INSPECTION: Buyer may order an inspection report dated within 7 days of date of this contract, by a licensed termite inspector. Any damage or infestation found may be corrected at seller's expense, or at their option the sellers may terminate this contract (unless buyer elects to accept property in its then condition) and refund the deposit to the buyers.

EXPENSES: Seller shall pay for the preparation of the note(s), mortgage(s) and deed and for the recording of the deed and the documentary stamps on the deed. Buyer shall pay for the intangible tax and for the documentary stamps on the note(s) and mortgages(s).

PRORATION OF TAXES: Real property taxes shall be prorated based on the current year's tax.

INSURANCE: Purchaser to obtain hazard insurance for an amount sufficient to replace the structure in the event of fire or other damage, and to name holders of secured loans as additional loss payees.

CONDITION: Buyer(s) have the right to have the house inspected at their expense and to furnish the seller with a list of any deficiencies within fifteen days of the date of this contract. The seller shall repair any deficiencies before the closing to the satisfaction of the buyer.

POSSESSION: Possession shall be delivered to the Buyer upon recordation of the deed.

RISK OF LOSS: Risk of loss due to fire or other casualty shall remain with the Seller until title transfers. In the event of insurable loss, buyer has the option to close and receive the proceeds of any insurance payment.

DEFAULT: In the event Buyer defaults hereunder, the Buyer shall forfeit his deposit as full liquidated damages. In the event seller defaults, buyer shall be entitled to a refund of their deposit, plus any actual expenses incurred by the buyer as a result of this transaction and buyer may pursue any remedies under law including a suit for specific performance. The buyer shall be entitled to any attorney's fees incurred as a result of enforcing this contract.

RADON GAS: Radon is a naturally occurring radioactive gas that, when it has accumulated in a building in sufficient quantities, may present health risks to persons who are exposed to it over time. Levels of radon that exceed federal and state guidelines have been found in buildings in this state. Information regarding radon and radon testing may be obtained from your county public health unit.

Appendix

LEAD PAINT: Every purchaser of any interest in residential real property built prior to 1978 is notified that such property may present exposure to lead from lead based paint that may place young children at risk of developing lead poisoning. Lead poisoning in young children may produce permanent neurological damage, including learning disabilities, reduced intelligence quotient, behavioral problems, and impaired memory. Lead poisoning also poses a particular risk to pregnant women. The seller of any interest in residential real property is required to provide the buyer with any information on lead-based paint hazards from risk assessments or inspections in the sellers possession and notify the buyer of any known lead based paint hazards. A risk assessment or inspection for possible lead based paint hazards is recommended prior to the purchase. Sellers acknowledge the receipt of the booklet titled "Protect Your Family From Lead Paint In Your Home".

ACCEPTANCE: This instrument shall become a binding contract when signed by both Buyer and Seller. If it is not accepted and signed by the Seller prior to _____, 20_____ this contract shall be void.

CLOSING: Closing shall take place on or before _____, 20_____ at a title company of buyers choosing.

OTHER AGREEMENTS: No prior or representations shall be binding upon the parties hereto unless incorporated in this contract.

TIME IS OF THE ESSENCE of this agreement. Each party shall diligently pursue the completion of this transaction.
OTHER TERMS AND CONDITIONS:

THIS IS A LEGALLY BINDING CONTRACT! IF NOT FULLY UNDERSTOOD, SEEK LEGAL ADVICE BEFORE SIGNING.

SIGNED, sealed and delivered this _____day of _____, 2000

_____   _____
Witness   Buyer

_____   _____
Witness   Buyer

ACCEPTED, signed, sealed and delivered this_____ day of _____, 20_____

_____   _____
Witness   Seller

Appendix

The following addendum can be used with a Realtor's contract or any contract that favors the seller

Addendum To Purchase Contract

This will modify the contract dated _____20__ between buyers:_____
and sellers:_____
regarding property located at:_____

1. The earnest money deposit shall be paid to:_____ within 48 hours of acceptance of this contract by the sellers.

2. Buyer shall take title subject to the existing loans previously recited in this contract, on terms agreeable to the buyer. In the event that amount of the existing loans on the contract is misstated, then any overstatement shall be added to the purchase money note and any understatement will be deducted from the down payment.

3. Taxes and insurance impound accounts are included in the purchase price and shall be assigned to buyer at closing. Any shortage in these accounts will be charged to seller at closing. Seller agrees to sign a limited power of attorney giving the buyer the right to negotiate any refunded escrow funds.

4. The following personal property will be transferred by bill of sale at closing, free and clear of all encumbrances.

5. In the event the buyer defaults on this contract, the seller agrees to accept the earnest money deposit as full liquidated damages. Should the seller default, the seller agrees to pay for buyers expenses paid, including costs of inspections, title examination, appraisals and legal fees.

6. Seller agrees to permit the buyer the right to advertise, place signs on the property, and show the property after the contract is accepted and before the closing.

Appendix

7. Sellers agree that the buyer may have access to the property and have permission to make improvements prior to closing. In the event buyers fail to close, these improvements will become the property of sellers without compensation to the buyers.

8. Buyers have the right to have the property inspected at their expense. Should the inspection reveal any defects, the buyers at their option can void this offer or notify the sellers who will have until closing to correct such defect to the satisfaction of the buyer.

9. In the event of a dispute, parties agree to submit to first mediation and then binding arbitration.

Signed this _____ day of _____ 20_____

Sellers:_____ Buyers:_____

Appendix

Example of a Bank Contract used to sell bank owned property

CONTRACT FOR SALE OF REAL ESTATE

This agreement, made this _____ day of _____, 20_____, between <u>ABC COMPANIES LENDING CORPORATION</u>, as "Seller" and _____, as "Purchaser" provides:

1. That the Seller agrees to sell and convey to the Purchaser and the Purchaser agrees to buy and take the following described property

_____

_____

whose street address is: _____

2. The Purchase Price is _____

payable as follows: _____

_____

_____

3. The Purchaser has paid to the Seller a deposit of \$_____, receipt of which is hereby acknowledged by the Seller and shall be applied to the first installment of the purchase price. The Purchaser's obligation thereunder is conditional on the Seller's ability to convey marketable title. If the Seller is unable to provide marketable title, the deposit shall be returned to the Purchaser and all rights and liabilities will be terminated.

4. The Purchaser acknowledges that they have received the attached lead based paint warning statement, they further acknowledge that pursuant to Title 12 of the USC and the implementing regulations, the attached contract entitles them to 10 calendar days to contact a risk management or inspection. The Purchaser also has the option to agree to the following:

Please initial and date if applicable

_____ The purchaser hereby agrees to waive their right to the aforesaid inspection.

_____ The Purchaser and Seller mutually agree to reduce the allotted time for said inspection period.

The inspection period is to begin on _____ and end on _____.

Appendix

5.   Seller agrees to convey title to the aforesaid property to the Purchaser by Special Warranty Deed, Warranty, Deed, or Quit Claim Deed, free and clear of all encumbrances and/or liens. Seller shall be allowed a reasonable time to examine title and if necessary, correct and title obligations. Subject to the aforesaid curative period. THIS SALE SHOULD BE CLOSED ON OR BEFORE _____. 20_____

6.   Improvements shall be in substantially the same condition on the date of settlement as on the date of this agreement. Purchaser accepts the property in its current condition, without any improvements or repairs. Purchaser further acknowledges that a full and complete inspection was made of the premises and that they are buying subject to all defects both apparent and hidden, THE PROPERTY IS SOLD IN THE "AS IS" CONDITION WITH NO WARRANTIES EXPRESSED OR IMPLIED.

7.   Mortgage Title Insurance will be paid by the ____ Purchaser ____ Seller. *Owner's* Title Insurance will be the *option* of the Purchaser and at the expense of the ____ Purchaser ____ Seller .

8.   Taxes shall be prorated as of the date of the actual settlement. All other Closing Costs shall be divided as follows:
Purchaser: _____

Seller: _____

9.   The Seller agrees to pay a Broker/Real Estate Agent a sum equal to _____ % of the "As Is" Purchase Price of $_____ as commission at the time of sale. Commission WILL NOT be paid on repairs done to the property.

_____   _____
Witness to Purchaser's Signature   Purchaser

_____   _____
Witness to Purchaser's Signature   Purchaser

_____   _____
Seller as Agent for ABC COMPANIES   Date
LENDING CORPORATION

Appendix

Can be used when buying and taking title" Subject To" existing loans

Limited Power of Attorney

This day_____, identified as the current owner and hereinafter referred to as "Owner" of the property located at _____, and is the same person who owes money on a loan with _____, hereinafter referred to as "Lender", Loan # _____, which is secured by a mortgage on the property noted above.

The Owner states that (s)he is in default on the loan and that foreclosure procedures have been brought by the above lender.

In order to resolve this situation,_____, hereafter called the Buyer, or his assignees, will buy the house and resolve all payments due to the Lender stated above, and take title to the property subject to the above stated loans.

As part of this solution, and in consideration for benefits to him(her), the Owner(s) give to Buyer a limited power of attorney to act for him/her in the following manner:

Specifically, the Owner appoints the Buyer, his/her Attorney in Fact to negotiate any agreement with the lender, and fully resolve and settle how funds in the escrow account should be applied or paid out of the escrow account. In the event that any funds are released or paid out of the escrow fund in regard to this property,_____ as Attorney in Fact can sign or endorse the check on behalf of the Owner, and apply or use the funds as Buyer solely determines.

WITNESS my hand and seal the _____day of _____, 20____ in _____ County, Florida.

Appendix

Witness: Owner(s):

_____   _____

_____   _____

STATE OF_____

COUNTY OF_____

    I HEREBY CERTIFY that on this day, before me, an officer duly authorized in the State aforesaid and in the County aforesaid to take acknowledgments, personally appeared _____ the Owner(s), to me known to be the person described in and who executed the foregoing instrument and he acknowledged before me that he executed the same.

WITNESS my hand and official seal in the County and State last aforesaid This _____ day of _____ 20____

_____

Notary Public, State of _____

Appendix

A. Settlement Statement　　　　**U.S. Department of Housing and Urban Development**　　　　OMB No. 2502-0265

B. Type of Loan					
1. ☐ FHA 2. ☐ FmHA 3. ☐ Conv Unins	6. File Number R07028411		7. Loan Number	8. Mortgage Ins Case Number	
4. ☐ VA 5. ☐ Conv Ins. 6. ☐ Seller Finance					

C. Note: This form is furnished to give you a statement of actual settlement costs. Amounts paid to and by the settlement agent are shown. Items marked "(p.o.c.)" were paid outside the closing; they are shown here for informational purposes and are not included in the totals.

D. Name & Address of Borrower	E. Name & Address of Seller	F. Name & Address of Lender
Ronald Roggow 5523 Briarcliff Sarasota, FL 34232	Deutsche Bank National Trust Company, as Trustee for the Certificateholders of Soundview Home Loan Trust 2005-OPT4, Asset-Backed Certificates, Series 2005-OPT4	CASH

G. Property Location	H. Settlement Agent Name
Ridgewood Estates 17th Addition, Lot 883, Sarasota County 5523 Briarcliffe DR Sarasota, FL 34232	New House Title, L.L.C. 9119 Corporate Lake Drive, Suite 300 Tampa, FL 33634 Tax ID: 04-3814236

Place of Settlement	I. Settlement Date
New House Title, L.L.C. 9119 Corporate Lake Drive, Suite 300 Tampa, FL 33634	03/26/2008 Fund:

J. Summary of Borrower's Transaction		K. Summary of Seller's Transaction	
100. Gross Amount Due from Borrower		**400. Gross Amount Due to Seller**	
101. Contract Sales Price	$120,000.00	401. Contract Sales Price	$120,000.00
102. Personal Property		402. Personal Property	
103. Settlement Charges to borrower	$268.50	403.	
104.		404.	
105.		405.	
Adjustments for items paid by seller in advance		Adjustments for items paid by seller in advance	
106. County property taxes		406. County property taxes	
107. HOA		407. HOA	
108. Condo Assoc.		408. Condo Assoc.	
109. Non Ad-Valorem		409. Non Ad-Valorem	
110. .		410. .	
111. .		411. .	
112.		412.	
113.		413.	
114.		414.	
115.		415.	
116.		416.	
120. Gross Amount Due From Borrower	$120,268.50	**420. Gross Amount Due to Seller**	$120,000.00
200. Amounts Paid By Or in Behalf Of Borrower		**500. Reductions in Amount Due to Seller**	
201. Deposit or earnest money	$1,000.00	501. Excess Deposit	
202. Principal amount of new loan(s)		502. Settlement Charges to Seller (line 1400)	$9,160.00
203. Existing loan(s) taken subject to		503. Existing Loan(s) Taken Subject to	
204. Commitment fee		504. Payoff of first mortgage loan	
205.		505. Payoff of second mortgage loan	
206.		506.	
207.		507.	
208.		508.	
209.		509.	
Adjustments for items unpaid by seller		Adjustments for items unpaid by seller	
210. County property taxes 01/01/08 thru 03/25/08	$574.95	510. County property taxes 01/01/08 thru 03/25/08	$574.95
211. HOA		511. HOA	
212. Condo Assoc.		512. Condo Assoc.	
213. Non Ad-Valorem		513. Non Ad-Valorem	
214. .		514. .	
215. .		515. .	
216.		516.	
217.		517.	
218.		518.	
219.		519.	
220. Total Paid By/For Borrower	$1,574.95	**520. Total Reduction Amount Due Seller**	$9,734.95
300. Cash At Settlement From/To Borrower		**600. Cash At Settlement To/From Seller**	
301. Gross Amount due from borrower (line 120)	$120,268.50	601. Gross Amount due to seller (line 420)	$120,000.00
302. Less amounts paid by/for borrower (line 220)	$1,574.95	602. Less reductions in amt. due seller (line 520)	$9,734.95
303. Cash From Borrower	$118,693.55	**603. Cash To Seller**	$110,265.05

Section 5 of the Real Estate Settlement Procedures Act (RESPA) requires the following: • HUD must develop a Special Information Booklet to help persons borrowing money to finance the purchase of residential real estate to better understand the nature and costs of real estate settlement services;
• Each lender must provide the booklet to all applicants from whom it receives or for whom it prepares a written application to borrow money to finance the purchase of residential real estate; • Lenders must prepare and distribute with the Booklet a Good Faith Estimate of the settlement costs that the borrower is likely to incur in connection with the settlement. These disclosures are mandatory.

Section 4(a) of RESPA mandates that HUD develop and prescribe this standard form to be used at the time of loan settlement to provide full disclosure of all charges imposed upon the borrower and seller. These are third party disclosures that are designed to provide the borrower with pertinent information during the settlement process in order to be a better shopper.
The Public Reporting Burden for this collection of information is estimated to average one hour per response, including the time for reviewing instructions, searching existing data sources, gathering and maintaining the data needed, and completing and reviewing the collection of information.
This agency may not collect this information, and you are not required to complete this form, unless it displays a currently valid OMB control number. The information requested does not lend itself to confidentiality.

Appendix

L. Settlement Charges				Paid From Borrower's Funds at Settlement	Paid From Seller's Funds at Settlement
700. Total Sales/Broker's Commission based on price	$120,000.00	@ % = $5,400.00			
Division of Commission (line 700) as follows:					
701. $2,700.00	to	Coldwell Banker Residential Real Estate			
702. $2,700.00	to	Coldwell Banker			
703. Commission Paid at Settlement				$0.00	$5,400.00
704. Shared Commission	to	First Option Asset Management Services			$1,800.00
800. Items Payable in Connection with Loan					
801. Loan Origination Fee %	to				
802. Loan Discount %	to				
803. Appraisal Fee	to				
804. Credit Report	to				
805. Lender's Inspection Fee	to				
806. Mortgage Insurance Application	to				
807. Assumption Fee	to				
808. Flood Certification Fee	to				
809. Processing Fee	to				
810. Tax Service Fee	to				
811. Broker Fee	to				
812. Premium Yld Sprd	to				
900. Items Required by Lender To Be Paid in Advance					
901. Interest from	to	@ /day			
902. Mortgage Insurance Premium for months	to				
903. Hazard Insurance Premium for years	to				
1000. Reserves Deposited With Lender					
1001. Hazard insurance	months @	per month			
1002. Mortgage insurance	months @	per month			
1003. County property taxes	months @	per month			
1004. HOA	months @	per month			
1005. Condo Assoc.	months @	per month			
1006. Non Ad-Valorem	months @	per month			
1007.	months @	per month			
1008.	months @	per month			
1011. Aggregate Adjustment					
1100. Title Charges				$200.00	$125.00
1101. Settlement or closing fee	to	New House Title, L.L.C.			
1102. Abstract or title search	to	New House Title, L.L.C.			$200.00
1103. Title examination	to	New House Title, L.L.C.			
1104. Title insurance binder	to				
1105. Document preparation	to				
1106. Notary fees	to				
1107. Attorney's fees	to				
(includes above items numbers:		)			
1108. Title insurance	to	New House Title, L.L.C.			$675.00
(includes above items numbers:		)			
1109. Lender's coverage	$0.00/$0.00				
1110. Owner's coverage	$120,000.00/$675.00				
1111. Endorse:	to	New House Title, L.L.C.			
1112. Municipal Lien Search and Review-PDR	to	New House Title, L.L.C.			$120.00
1113. Record Retention	to	New House Title, L.L.C.		$50.00	
1114. Courtesy Closing Fee (POC by NHT)	to	KC Signing, LLC	POC $150.00		
1200. Government Recording and Transfer Charges					
1201. Recording Fees	Deed $18.50 ; Mortgage ; Rel	to Sarasota County Clerk of Courts		$18.50	
1202. City/county tax/stamps	Deed ; Mortgage	to			
1203. State tax/stamps	Deed $840.00 ; Mortgage	to Sarasota County Clerk of Courts			$840.00
1204. Record Power of Attorney	to				
1300. Additional Settlement Charges					
1301. Survey	to				
1302. Pest Inspection	to				
1303. Home Protection Plan	to				
1304. 2007 R.E. Taxes	to	Sarasota County Tax Collector	POC $2,394.83		
1400. Total Settlement Charges (enter on lines 103, Section J and 502, Section K)				$268.50	$9,160.00

I have carefully reviewed the HUD-1 Settlement Statement and to the best of my knowledge and belief, it is a true and accurate statement of all receipts and disbursements made on my account or by me in this transaction. I further certify that I have received a completed copy of pages 1, 2 and 3 of this HUD-1 Settlement Statement.

Deutsche Bank National Trust Company, As Trustee

Ronald Roggow

By _____

SETTLEMENT AGENT CERTIFICATION
The HUD-1 Settlement Statement which I have prepared is a true and accurate account of this transaction. I have caused the funds to be disbursed in accordance with this statement.

Settlement Agent _____ Date _____

Warning: It is a crime to knowingly make false statements to the United States on this or any other similar form. Penalties upon conviction can include a fine and imprisonment. For details see: Title 18 U.S. Code Section 1001 and Section 1010.

Appendix

A. **Settlement Statement**

U.S. Department of Housing
and Urban Development

OMB Approval No. 2502-0265
(expires 11/30/2009)

B. Type of Loan

					6. File Number:	7. Loan Number:	8. Mortgage Insurance Case Number:
1. ☐ FHA	2. ☐ FmHA	3. ☐ Conv. Unins.					
4. ☐ VA	5. ☐ Conv. Ins.						

C. Note: This form is furnished to give you a statement of actual settlement costs. Amounts paid to and by the settlement agent are shown. Items marked "(p.o.c.)" were paid outside the closing; they are shown here for informational purposes and are not included in the totals.

D. Name & Address of Borrower:	E. Name & Address of Seller:	F. Name & Address of Lender:

G. Property Location:	H. Settlement Agent:	
	Place of Settlement:	I. Settlement Date:

J. Summary of Borrower's Transaction		**K. Summary of Seller's Transaction**	
100. Gross Amount Due From Borrower		**400. Gross Amount Due To Seller**	
101. Contract sales price		401. Contract sales price	
102. Personal property		402. Personal property	
103. Settlement charges to borrower (line 1400)		403.	
104.		404.	
105.		405.	
Adjustments for items paid by seller in advance		**Adjustments for items paid by seller in advance**	
106. City/town taxes to		406. City/town taxes to	
107. County taxes to		407. County taxes to	
108. Assessments to		408. Assessments to	
109.		409.	
110.		410.	
111.		411.	
112.		412.	
120. Gross Amount Due From Borrower		**420. Gross Amount Due To Seller**	
200. Amounts Paid By Or In Behalf Of Borrower		**500. Reductions In Amount Due To Seller**	
201. Deposit or earnest money		501. Excess deposit (see instructions)	
202. Principal amount of new loan(s)		502. Settlement charges to seller (line 1400)	
203. Existing loan(s) taken subject to		503. Existing loan(s) taken subject to	
204.		504. Payoff of first mortgage loan	
205.		505. Payoff of second mortgage loan	
206.		506.	
207.		507.	
208.		508.	
209.		509.	
Adjustments for items unpaid by seller		**Adjustments for items unpaid by seller**	
210. City/town taxes to		510. City/town taxes to	
211. County taxes to		511. County taxes to	
212. Assessments to		512. Assessments to	
213.		513.	
214.		514.	
215.		515.	
216.		516.	
217.		517.	
218.		518.	
219.		519.	
220. Total Paid By/For Borrower		**520. Total Reduction Amount Due Seller**	
300. Cash At Settlement From/To Borrower		**600. Cash At Settlement To/From Seller**	
301. Gross Amount due from borrower (line 120)		601. Gross amount due to seller (line 420)	
302. Less amounts paid by/for borrower (line 220)	( )	602. Less reductions in amt. due seller (line 520)	( )
303. Cash ☐ From ☐ To Borrower		**603. Cash** ☐ To ☐ From Seller	

Section 5 of the Real Estate Settlement Procedures Act (RESPA) requires the following: • HUD must develop a Special Information Booklet to help persons borrowing money to finance the purchase of residential real estate to better understand the nature and costs of real estate settlement services; • Each lender must provide the booklet to all applicants from whom it receives or for whom it prepares a written application to borrow money to finance the purchase of residential real estate; • Lenders must prepare and distribute with the Booklet a Good Faith Estimate of the settlement costs that the borrower is likely to incur in connection with the settlement. These disclosures are manadatory.

Section 4(a) of RESPA mandates that HUD develop and prescribe this standard form to be used at the time of loan settlement to provide full disclosure of all charges imposed upon the borrower and seller. These are third party disclosures that are designed to provide the borrower with pertinent information during the settlement process in order to be a better shopper.

The Public Reporting Burden for this collection of information is estimated to average one hour per response, including the time for reviewing instructions, searching existing data sources, gathering and maintaining the data needed, and completing and reviewing the collection of information.

This agency may not collect this information, and you are not required to complete this form, unless it displays a currently valid OMB control number. The information requested does not lend itself to confidentiality.

Appendix

L. Settlement Charges

		Paid From Borrowers Funds at Settlement	Paid From Seller's Funds at Settlement
700. Total Sales/Broker's Commission based on price $ @ % =			
Division of Commission (line 700) as follows:			
701. $ to			
702. $ to			
703. Commission paid at Settlement			
704.			
800. Items Payable In Connection With Loan			
801. Loan Origination Fee %			
802. Loan Discount %			
803. Appraisal Fee to			
804. Credit Report to			
805. Lender's Inspection Fee			
806. Mortgage Insurance Application Fee to			
807. Assumption Fee			
808.			
809.			
810.			
811.			
900. Items Required By Lender To Be Paid In Advance			
901. Interest from to @$ /day			
902. Mortgage Insurance Premium for months to			
903. Hazard Insurance Premium for years to			
904. years to			
905.			
1000. Reserves Deposited With Lender			
1001. Hazard insurance months @$ per month			
1002. Mortgage insurance months @$ per month			
1003. City property taxes months @$ per month			
1004. County property taxes months @$ per month			
1005. Annual assessments months @$ per month			
1006. months @$ per month			
1007. months @$ per month			
1008. months @$ per month			
1100. Title Charges			
1101. Settlement or closing fee to			
1102. Abstract or title search to			
1103. Title examination to			
1104. Title insurance binder to			
1105. Document preparation to			
1106. Notary fees to			
1107. Attorney's fees to			
(includes above items numbers:)			
1108. Title insurance to			
(includes above items numbers:)			
1109. Lender's coverage $			
1110. Owner's coverage $			
1111.			
1112.			
1113.			
1200. Government Recording and Transfer Charges			
1201. Recording fees: Deed $; Mortgage $; Releases $			
1202. City/county tax/stamps: Deed $; Mortgage $			
1203. State tax/stamps: Deed $; Mortgage $			
1204.			
1205.			
1300. Additional Settlement Charges			
1301. Survey to			
1302. Pest inspection to			
1303.			
1304.			
1305.			
1400. Total Settlement Charges (enter on lines 103, Section J and 502, Section K)			

The Undersigned Acknowledges Receipt of this Disclosure Statement and Agrees to the Correctness Thereof.

_____   _____

_____   _____

Buyer or Agent   Seller or Agent

Index

Index

Index

Index

Index

Index

Index

Index

Index

Index

About the Author

Helping property owners in trouble is John Schaub's specialty. His buying business is entirely referral, as he does not advertise. In 35 years of buying property in the same town, he has helped many who have in turn sent him more business.

Working smart allows John to work less than he plays. He spends more time sailing or flying his plane to his favorite fishing or dive location, than sitting behind a desk.

He is an active participant in building affordable housing in his town and worldwide. For 23 years he has served on his local Habitat for Humanity Board, plus another 7 years on the Habitat International Board. He currently serves on the Board of Habitat Sarasota, plus the Fuller Center for Housing and other local nonprofit boards. He encourages others to give back.

John continues to teach several classes a year in which students actually find and make offers on houses at bargain prices. In addition, John writes a national newsletter on real estate investing called *Strategies and Solutions*.

For John's speaking schedule and to see a copy of his newsletter go to www.johnschaub.com.